Items should be returned on or before
shown below. Items not already reque
borrowers may be renewed in person,
telephone. To renew, please quote the number on the
barcode label. To renew online a PIN is required.
This can be requested at your local library.
Renew online @ **www.dublincitypubliclibraries.ie**
Fines charged for overdue items will include postage
incurred in recovery. Damage to or loss of items will
be charged to the borrower.

Leabharlanna Poiblí Chathair Bhaile Átha Cliath
Dublin City Public Libraries

Date Due	Date Due	Date Due

f
d
ble

KQA
red
v

Your
com

ut

Ltd

s

mer
nool

his

DIS

/

PR

d
all

insights into how these people have used innovation to achieve amazing
*things in their respective fields. Perhaps you will be inspired to become
more innovative too...'*
**Iain Bitran, Executive Director, ISPIM - International Society for
Professional Innovation Management**

THINK LIKE AN
INNOVATOR

PEARSON

At Pearson, we believe in learning – all kinds of learning for all kinds of people. Whether it's at home, in the classroom or in the workplace, learning is the key to improving our life chances.

That's why we're working with leading authors to bring you the latest thinking and the best practices, so you can get better at the things that are important to you. You can learn on the page or on the move, and with content that's always crafted to help you understand quickly and apply what you've learned.

If you want to upgrade your personal skills or accelerate your career, become a more effective leader or more powerful communicator, discover new opportunities or simply find more inspiration, we can help you make progress in your work and life.

Every day our work helps learning flourish, and wherever learning flourishes, so do people.

To learn more please visit us at: www.pearson.com/uk

THINK LIKE AN
INNOVATOR

76 inspiring business lessons from the world's greatest thinkers and innovators

Paul Sloane

PEARSON

Harlow, England • London • New York • Boston • San Francisco • Toronto • Sydney
Auckland • Singapore • Hong Kong • Tokyo • Seoul • Taipei • New Delhi
Cape Town • São Paulo • Mexico City • Madrid • Amsterdam • Munich • Paris • Milan

PEARSON EDUCATION LIMITED
Edinburgh Gate
Harlow CM20 2JE
United Kingdom
Tel: +44 (0)1279 623623
Web: www.pearson.com/uk

First published 2016 (print and electronic)

ISBN: 978-1-292-14223-4 (print)
       978-1-292-14224-1 (PDF)
       978-1-292-14225-8 (ePub)

British Library Cataloguing-in-Publication Data
A catalogue record for the print edition is available from the British Library

Library of Congress Cataloging-in-Publication Data
A catalog record for the print edition is available from the Library of Congress

10 9 8 7 6 5 4 3 2 1
19 18 17 16

Text design by Design Deluxe

Cover design by Two Associates

Print edition typeset in 9.5/14pt Helvetica by iEnergizer Aptara®, Ltd

Printed in Great Britain by Ashford Colour Press Ltd.

NOTE THAT ANY PAGE CROSS REFERENCES REFER TO THE PRINT EDITION

CONTENTS

About the author xi

Introduction xiii

Part 1 Artist

David Bowie 3

Freddie Mercury 6

Hans Christian Andersen 10

J.K. Rowling 13

John Lennon and Paul McCartney 16

Madonna 19

Miles Davis 23

Pablo Picasso 26

Roy Lichtenstein 29

Salvador Dali 32

Woody Allen 35

Part 2 Business leader

Akio Morita 41

Anne Mulcahy 45

Clarence Birdseye 49

Daniel Peter   52

Ingvar Kamprad   55

Jeff Bezos   58

Levi Strauss   62

Ray Kroc   65

Ricardo Semler   68

Rob McEwen   72

Sidney Bernstein   75

Sir Charles Dunstone   78

Soichiro Honda   81

Zhang Ruimin   84

Part 3 Genius

Ludwig van Beethoven   89

Michelangelo   93

Mozart   97

Pythagoras   100

William Shakespeare   103

Part 4 Inventor

Eric Migicovsky   109

George de Mestral   112

Sir Hiram Maxim   115

Johannes Gutenberg   118

John Harrison   121

John Sipe   126

Jorge Odón   129

Louis Braille   132

Martin Cooper   136

Nick D'Aloisio   140

Percy Spencer   143

Ted Hoff   146

Thomas Edison   149

Trevor Baylis   152

Part 5 Maverick

Anita Roddick   159

Don Estridge   163

Hannibal   167

Viscount Horatio Nelson   170

Jonathan Swift   173

Phil Romano   177

Steve Jobs   180

Part 6 Pioneer

Auguste Escoffier   185

Dick Fosbury   188

Florence Nightingale   191

Guglielmo Marconi   195

Gustave Eiffel   198

Hedy Lamarr   202

Muhammad Yunus   206

Travis Kalanick   210

Part 7 Scientist

Sir Alexander Fleming   215

Alexander Graham Bell   218

Archimedes   222

Charles Darwin   225

Dmitri Mendeleev   229

Edward Jenner   232

Edwin Land   235

Galileo   238

Govindappa Venkataswamy   242

Joseph Lister   245

Marie Curie   248

Part 8 Visionary

Elon Musk   253

John F. Kennedy   256

Mahatma Gandhi   259

Oprah Winfrey   262

Walt Disney   265

Zhao Kuangyin   268

Index   271

ABOUT THE AUTHOR

Paul Sloane studied Engineering at Cambridge University. He was a top salesman with IBM and went on to be Marketing Director, Managing Director and CEO of software companies. He is the author of over 25 books on leadership, innovation, lateral thinking and puzzles. He is a renowned speaker and course leader and a prolific blogger with over 30,000 followers on Twitter (@paulsloane). He and his wife live in Camberley, Surrey. They have three daughters.

INTRODUCTION

Everyone needs, at some time or other, to be an innovator. And everyone can be. You just have to think like an innovator and act like one. But most of us find this difficult. There is a natural tendency to avoid undue risks, to repeat what worked in the past and to settle for a comfortable life. This book aims to give you the inspiration and insights to break out of your comfort zone and to try new adventures. It consists of short stories drawn from the lives of great innovators from different ages and fields. They have been chosen not because they represent the best or most representative group. They have been chosen because of the variety of lessons and insights they illustrate. Inevitably, there will be some overlap in the precepts that we draw from these examples but, nonetheless, there is a great diversity there, too.

There are eight categories of innovators, including artists, inventors, scientists and business leaders. Some listings were easy to categorise but some like, say, Elon Musk could have fallen into any of three categories. What can a business executive learn from an artist? Or a musician from a warrior? Or a teacher from an athlete? The answer is much. It has been observed that, on problem solving sites like Innocentive.com, the person who offers the best solution for a challenge usually comes from a very different field from the person who posed the question.

The book is designed to be dipped into. It does not need to be read sequentially. One suggested approach is this. Start with a challenge or problem that needs an innovative solution. Ponder the challenge without trying to solve it. Now read about one of the great innovators in this book. Apply the insights listed at the end of the chapter to the issue. How might the character from the book have tackled the problem you face? If he or she cannot help, try another until you get the inspiration you need. There are over 200 separate insights in the book, so it is likely that help is at hand somewhere.

If your favourite innovator is not on the list, if you spot any factual error or, if you want to add a comment about the book, simply search on Facebook for Think Like an Innovator. You can share your thoughts there. I will be getting involved, too, and your ideas might well inform the next edition.

PART 1
ARTIST

DAVID BOWIE

(1947 – 2016)

Influential musician, style
icon and creative collaborator

David Bowie was a singer, songwriter, multi-instrumentalist, record producer, arranger, painter and actor. He was a highly influential musician who continually reinvented his sound and persona, from the 1960s hippy of Space Oddity, through Ziggy Stardust, Aladdin Sane, Pierrot, Thin White Duke and into an elder statesman of soulful rock. His varied androgynous appearances influenced fashion and changed attitudes towards bisexuality.

Many of his innovations sprang from his numerous collaborations. He acknowledged the influence of the Legendary Stardust Cowboy, a Texan singer, and, in particular, his single 'Paralyzed', which Bowie described as 'the most awful cacophony.' However, it helped to form Bowie's first great persona, Ziggy Stardust.

In the 1970s, he worked with Lou Reed and produced Reed's great hit, 'Transformer'. He collaborated with Iggy Pop on two albums, thus launching Pop's solo career. He subsequently teamed up with Bruce Springsteen and then Luther Vandross with whom he co-wrote the big hit, 'Young Americans', which launched another new style, plastic soul. Lou Reed, Iggy Pop, Springsteen and Vandross all benefitted from working with Bowie and went on to achieve individual success.

Bowie's first US number one single, 'Fame', was co-written with John Lennon and Carlos Alomar. In the late 1970s, Bowie moved to Berlin and joined forces with Brian Eno, formerly of Roxy Music. They incorporated Euro-disco, punk and German art-rock music into three landmark albums.

In the years that followed, Bowie continued to explore new themes and styles. He collaborated with Nile Rodgers, Mick Jagger, Queen and even Bing Crosby.

During the 1970s, Bowie developed an acting career, starring in Nicolas Roeg's film *The Man Who Fell to Earth*. He created many startling music videos. In the 1980s, he became a stage actor playing the lead in *The Elephant Man* on Broadway. In 2006, he made a surprise return to film, playing Nikola Tesla in Christopher Nolan's illusionist drama *The Prestige*.

His final album, the critically acclaimed *Blackstar*, which contained innovative jazz fusion elements, was released on his 69th birthday, just days before his death in 2016.

INSIGHTS FOR INNOVATORS

Be promiscuous in your collaborations. Bowie did not rely on his own genius; he constantly sought fresh stimuli by collaborating with different people. Most collaborations led to innovations in style and musical direction. He could easily have cruised along, simply recycling his early hits as many other aging rock stars do. Instead, he kept looking for fresh ideas – some of which surprised and annoyed his original fans but earned him new ones.

Impose change on yourself. Keep exploring new avenues. Bowie said, 'I feel confident imposing change on myself. It's a lot more fun progressing than looking back.'

DID YOU KNOW?... David Bowie was born David Jones in January 1947. He renamed himself in 1966 to avoid confusion with Davy Jones of The Monkees.

FREDDIE MERCURY

(1946 – 1991)

Pop's master showman

The song 'Bohemian Rhapsody' was written by Freddie Mercury for Queen's 1975 album, *A Night at the Opera*. It broke all the rules for a popular music single release. At a time when most pop songs were simple and formulaic, Mercury's song was a complex mixture of different styles and tempos. It had six separate sections – a close harmony *a capella* introduction, a ballad, a guitar solo, an opera parody, a rock anthem and a melodic finale. It contained enigmatic and fatalistic lyrics about killing a man. And it was very long.

When the band proposed to their record producers, EMI, that they release the song as a single, they flatly rejected the idea. It was 5 minutes 55 seconds in duration and the general rule of the day was that radio stations only played items that lasted no more than three and a half minutes.

So, Mercury bypassed EMI and went straight to his friend, the DJ Kenny Everett. He gave him a copy on condition that the DJ play only sections of it. There was still a concern that it was too long and complex for pop radio. Everett initially did this, but the reaction was so strong that he played the whole six minutes several times on his weekend show on Capital Radio. On the following Monday morning, hordes of fans went into music stores to buy the record, only to be told that it was not available. EMI was forced to release it and the song that they claimed was unplayable went on to become one of their greatest hits. It was the first song to reach number one twice with the same version – in 1975 on its first release and in 1991 following Mercury's death. It went gold in the USA, with over 1 million copies sold. It had a worldwide resurgence in 1992 when it featured in the film *Wayne's World*.

Freddie Mercury first started working on ideas for the song in the late 1960s. He did not write it to please customers or to follow a formula for a hit record. He wrote it as a creative piece of self-indulgent musical expression. It was fiendishly difficult to record with the equipment of the day. It was extremely risky in the nature of its composition and lyrics. Yet, in 2002, it was named by the *Guinness Book of Records* as the top British single of all time.

Freddie Mercury was born Farrokh Bulsara in 1946 in Zanzibar in East Africa (now part of Tanzania). His family were Parsis of Indian descent who practised the Zoroastrian religion. When he was 17, Farrokh and his family fled to England to avoid a revolution in Zanzibar in which thousands of Arabs and Indians were killed. Mercury studied Art at Isleworth Polytechnic on the outskirts of London. He joined a series of bands. In 1970, he met guitarist Brian May and drummer Roger Taylor. They formed a group for which Mercury chose the name 'Queen'. At about the same time, he changed his to Freddie Mercury. Queen went on to become one of the most important and influential rock bands of all time. Mercury wrote many of the band's greatest hits and he proved to be a brilliant front man on stage.

Mercury composed musically intricate songs that were also huge commercial hits. He defied conventions with unconventional arrangements featuring multiple key changes, obscure chords and strange harmonies. He experimented with a range of genres, including disco, dance, ragtime, opera and heavy rock.

Freddie Mercury died in 1991. In the years that followed, his recognition and popularity soared. In 1992, his tribute concert was held at Wembley Stadium, London. He was inducted into the Rock and Roll Hall of Fame in 2001, the Songwriters Hall of Fame in 2003 and the UK Music Hall of Fame in 2004. He was rated best male singer of all time in 2005 by Blender and MTV. A poll by Classic Rock in 2009 also voted him the best rock singer of all time.

INSIGHTS FOR INNOVATORS

Creative geniuses do not start by tinkering with what exists today. They do not listen to the demands of customers, bosses or critics. They start with their own revolutionary ideas and pursue them relentlessly. They do not work to the timetables, restrictions or expectations of others (even their own paymasters). They create their own masterpieces in their own time.

Sometimes, you have to be your own best showman to promote your unorthodox ideas and creations. If you truly believe in something, give it your best performance.

When conventional channels reject your work because it is too radical, then bypass them and go straight to the customer. As Mercury did with 'Bohemian Rhapsody'.

HANS CHRISTIAN ANDERSEN

(1805 – 1875)

Danish author of *Classic Fairy Tales*

H ans Christian Andersen was a prolific author who is famed for his fairy tales. Some of his most famous fairy tales include *The Emperor's New Clothes*, *Thumbelina*, *The Snow Queen*, *The Ugly Duckling*, *The Little Mermaid* and *The Princess and the Pea*. They have become popular with children and adults around the world and have inspired plays, films, cartoons and ballets.

Hans Christian Andersen was born in Odense in Denmark. He was the only child of a shoemaker and a washerwoman. They lived in poverty. His grandfather was assessed as mad and his grandmother worked as a gardener in a lunatic asylum. The young boy often visited her there and listened to the wild stories of the inmates.

Andersen's father introduced his son to the world of books, starting with the *Arabian Nights*. Following his father's death in 1816, Andersen was sent to a local school for poor children, where he was abused. He described his school years as the darkest and most bitter time of his life.

At 14, he moved to Copenhagen to seek work as an actor. He had an excellent soprano voice and was accepted into the Royal Danish Theatre. When his voice broke, he began to focus on writing. He produced novels, travelogues and poetry; and gained some slight recognition. In 1835, he started writing fairy stories. They showed a heroic struggle between good and evil and often they featured scary situations. Children loved them. They were translated into English and, gradually, became classic children's books. But their popularity was not limited to young readers. Their themes of virtue, courage, ingenuity and resilience made them enduring favourites with adults. They had a strong influence on playwrights and authors and in popular Western culture.

Andersen died in 1875, a Danish national hero. In 1913, a small bronze statue of a mermaid was unveiled on a rock in

Copenhagen harbour. The statue was commissioned by Carl Jacobsen after he saw a ballet version of Andersen's *The Little Mermaid*. It is a firm favourite with visitors to the city.

INSIGHTS FOR INNOVATORS

Mix with people from outside your comfort zone. If you mix with people like you, you will hear opinions like yours. Hans Christian Andersen went to a lunatic asylum to hear the stories of warders and inmates. They fuelled his imagination. He went on to create ingenious and inspirational fairy stories. Search out different, and even random, people, if you want different and radical ideas.

Give the people what they want. Andersen wanted to be a serious writer of novels and poetry, but he found that readers loved his fairy stories, so he developed those. He listened to his customers and gave them what they wanted.

DID YOU KNOW?... Disney Studios made an animated film version of one of Andersen's most cherished stories, *The Little Mermaid*. They changed the story to give it a happy ending – in contrast to the sad conclusion to the original tale. True fans of the author were disappointed at this treatment of a classic.

J.K. Rowling is the British author of the *Harry Potter* series of fantasy novels, which have become the best-selling book series in history with over 400 million copies sold. She acted as screenwriter and producer on the Harry Potter movies, which is the second highest-grossing film series ever.

Joanne Rowling was born in Gloucestershire in England in 1965. She worked as a researcher and secretary for the charity Amnesty International. In 1990, while on a delayed train journey, she had the idea of a young boy going to a school for wizards. But the next seven years were difficult for her. Her mother died of multiple sclerosis. Rowling moved to Portugal to teach English and there she met and married her husband. They had a daughter, but the marriage broke down and she fled with her child to Scotland. Her abusive husband followed her and she had to obtain a court order to keep him away. She lived as a jobless single mother on state benefits in relative poverty. She suffered from clinical depression and contemplated suicide. The script for her first book, *Harry Potter and the Philosopher's Stone*, was finished in 1995. She wrote it using an old manual typewriter.

The manuscript was rejected by 12 London publishing houses. After a year of unsuccessful attempts, she submitted it to the publisher Bloomsbury. The chairman of the company gave the first chapter of the manuscript to his eight-year-old daughter Alice, who loved it and demanded to read the next chapter. Bloomsbury agreed to publish the book, but advised Rowling to get a job, as she would never make money from writing children's books. The novel was published in 1997 and, the following year, it won the British Book Award for Children's Book of the Year. In the next 10 years, she wrote six sequels. The last four *Harry Potter* books each consecutively set records as the fastest-selling books in history.

The *Harry Potter* books became a global brand worth an estimated US$15 billion. They have been translated into

65 languages. The series is credited with reviving an interest in reading amongst a generation of children who previously had given up books in favour of computers and television.

INSIGHTS FOR INNOVATORS

The darkest hour is just before dawn. J.K. Rowling was at a very low ebb in her personal life, but continued to work at her dream. She wrote her first novel in cafés with her infant daughter asleep in a stroller beside her. She struggled to make ends meet, but is now one of the wealthiest women in Britain – she is also one of the most generous in her gifts to charities. If you are feeling depressed that your innovation is not succeeding, think of all the people who gave up too soon and those like Rowling who did not.

Rejection comes with the territory. Innovations break with conventions and, therefore, are hard to accept. Conventional publishers, all experts in their fields, saw no prospects in a book series that went on to sell 400 million copies. Do not let rejection get you down. *Gone with the Wind* by Margaret Mitchell was turned down 38 times. Skype, Google and Cisco were all rejected more than 30 times by investors on their initial pitches.

Is there a way to franchise your innovation? J.K. Rowling has written a series of books that then spun out into films, toys, clothing and many promotional items. How can you extend the reach and appeal of your new product to turn it into multiple revenue streams?

JOHN LENNON AND PAUL McCARTNEY

(1940 – 1980 AND BORN 1942)

The most successful songwriting partnership

The songwriting partnership between John Lennon and Paul McCartney of the Beatles is one of the most successful musical collaborations in history. Between 1962 and 1969, the pair published 180 jointly credited songs, mainly recorded by the Beatles and frequently covered by other artists.

Many songwriting partnerships consist of separate lyricist and composer, but Lennon and McCartney each wrote words and music. The two met as teenagers at a church fete in Liverpool in 1957. Lennon was playing with his skiffle group, the Quarrymen. He met McCartney and asked him to join the group. They formed the Beatles in 1960 together with George Harrison and (later) Ringo Starr. Lennon and McCartney were two creative prodigies who found that they could spur each other to write catchy songs. They decided that the songs they wrote, whether individually or together, should be credited to both of them.

Before they became famous, the Beatles played in clubs in Hamburg for two years. They performed live non-stop shows, sometimes for eight hours a day and seven days a week. When they were not playing, they practised, but not just by repeating the same songs. They constantly experimented and improvised.

Lennon and McCartney loved to meddle with each other's ideas. One would write a song and the other would suggest changes. They continually searched for new sounds, ideas and ways to make music. The Beatles were the first rock band to use feedback on 'I Feel Fine'. They used an Indian sitar on 'Revolver'. They used orchestral arrangements, double tracking and even played tapes backwards. Lennon and McCartney worked 'eyeball to eyeball'. They challenged each other, joked with each other and sometimes fell out. When one wrote a song, the other would add a riff, a different lyric or chord. A prominent example is the song 'A Day in the Life'. The main theme was written by Lennon. It starts with a sad refrain about reading the day's news. It needed something extra, so McCartney inserted a completely different song as an upbeat middle section about waking up and getting out of bed.

The Beatles became the best-selling music artists in the USA, with 178 million records sold. They have had more number-one albums in the British charts and sold more singles in the UK than any other act. In 2008, the Beatles were ranked number 1 in *Billboard* magazine's list of the all-time most successful artists.

INSIGHTS FOR INNOVATORS

Two and two can make five. Sometimes, in a really creative partnership, partners can spark off each other and be greater than the sum of its parts. The contention, rivalry and different styles that Lennon and McCartney brought to the pairing made their music truly extraordinary. They challenged each other, added ideas and went on an adventurous journey into unexplored territory. Find a partner who can bring out the best in you.

Practice makes perfect. By the time the Beatles became big stars in the USA in 1964, they had already played together over 1,200 times – more than most bands manage in their entire careers. Their dedication to rehearsal and performance made them relaxed yet consummately professional. It was the combination of the creative brilliance of the Lennon–McCartney partnership and the group's relentless work that made the Beatles the biggest band in rock music history.

DID YOU KNOW ?... John Lennon attended Quarry Bank High School in Liverpool. His school reports were very critical of him and included these comments, 'Certainly on the road to failure ... hopeless ... rather a clown in class ... wasting other pupils' time.' You do not need to be a great scholar to be a great innovator.

Madonna Louise Ciccone has sold over 300 million records worldwide and is recognised as the best-selling female recording artist of all time by Guinness World Records. She was born in 1958 in Bay City, Michigan. She attended the University of Michigan School of Music, Theatre & Dance before joining the group Breakfast Club where she sang and played drums and guitar. In 1981, she left the band to start a solo career. Her first album was titled *Madonna* and contained upbeat disco music. Her breakthrough came with her second album, *Like a Virgin*, in 1984. It was her first number one album and topped the charts in many countries. The catchy title track, 'Like a Virgin', was popular and controversial. It topped the Billboard Hot 100 chart for six weeks, but was criticised heavily by some who complained that the promotional video undermined marital values and promoted fornication.

Madonna continued to experiment with new styles of music and different artistic media. She changed her look with every new album. She started with pop and dance music in the 'Like a Virgin' style. Madonna's look and style of dressing was highly influential and she became a female fashion icon. Her look in the 1980s included bleached hair, lace tops, skirts over capri pants, fishnet stockings and heavy jewellery.

She changed her image and embraced Hollywood glamour as a 'Material Girl' in the style of Marilyn Monroe. In the 1990s, with 'Justify My Love' she pushed the boundaries of video towards S&M long before *Fifty Shades of Grey* came along. She has continued to innovate, provoke and court controversy with her music and videos while changing style and fashion. As a result, she became the most successful solo artist in the history of the US singles chart.

Madonna increased her reputation for versatility with her film roles. She appeared in the 1985 comedy *Desperately Seeking Susan* in which she sang 'Into the Groove', her first number one single in the United Kingdom. In 1996, she won a Golden

Globe Award for Best Actress for *Evita*. She has also enjoyed success with filmmaking, fashion design and writing children's books. As a highly successful businesswoman, Madonna founded entertainment company Maverick (including the label Maverick Records) in 1992 as a joint venture with Time Warner. In 2007, she signed a record $120 million deal with Live Nation.

Whilst there is no doubt that Madonna is an excellent songwriter, performer and lyricist, the longevity of her success is due to her powers of reinvention. Robert Grant, author of *Contemporary Strategy Analysis* (2005), commented that what has brought Madonna success involves combining the talents of others to help her numerous reincarnations. Madonna's approach was far from the music industry wisdom of 'Find a winning formula and stick to it.' Her musical career has been a continuous experimentation with new musical ideas and new images and a constant quest for new heights of fame and acclaim. Grant concluded that, 'having established herself as the queen of popular music, Madonna did not stop there, but continued reinventing.'

INSIGHTS FOR INNOVATORS

Get out of the groove and reinvent yourself. Once you break through with one success, do not just stick to what you are known for. Take risks and branch out in new directions. Madonna built on her initial success by continually taking on new challenges. Like David Bowie, she kept trying different approaches and different routes to market. As an innovator and leader, you should aim to recruit new followers continually by being innovative, topical and up-to-date.

▶

Do not copy trends, set them. Madonna is a fashion and music pioneer, not a follower. Examine currently popular styles and deliberately do something quite different.

Do not be afraid to upset people. Many complained that Madonna's videos and stage performances were distasteful. But her reputation as a rebel thrived on the hullabaloo. How can you harness provocation and controversy to promote your brand?

MILES DAVIS

(1926 – 1991)

Legendary jazz trumpeter, composer
and bandleader

M iles Davis is considered one of the most innovative and influential musicians of the twentieth century. Time and again, he changed the concept of jazz music. He was a leader in introducing bebop, a fast, improvisational style of jazz instrumental that defined the modern jazz era.

Davis was born in Alton, Illinois in 1926, the son of a dentist and a music teacher. At the age of 13, he was taught to play the trumpet by his father and the boy quickly showed a musical talent. As a teenager, he started to play professionally. When he was 17, he had a stroke of fortune. The eminent musicians Dizzy Gillespie and Charlie Parker needed a replacement trumpeter when their bandmate fell sick. They asked the young star to join them on stage and Davis was inspired by the experience. At the age of 18, he left home for New York where he studied at the Institute of Musical Art (now the Juilliard School) during the day and played in Harlem nightclubs at night.

He left the school and became a full-time musician, joining the Charlie Parker Quintet. He then formed his own band, the Miles Davis Sextet. He continuously developed his signature style of improvised trumpet playing.

In 1950, Davis became addicted to heroin. It took him four years to overcome his addiction. He assembled a ground-breaking band, which included John Coltrane, Paul Chambers and Red Garland. In 1959, he and the band recorded the seminal album, *Kind of Blue*, the best-selling jazz album of all time.

In the 1960s, he continued to transform his band and his music. He led the jazz fusion movement, which combined jazz with heavy rock. His *Bitches Brew* album became a best-selling example of this new genre of music. Davis was the first jazz musician to be featured on the front cover of *Rolling Stone*. This was too much for many conventional fans of traditional jazz, but Davis was more interested in pushing boundaries than pleasing fans.

During the 1970s, again he fell prey to addiction and submerged from view. Many fans thought he was finished but, to his credit, he reappeared with vigour in the 1980s. Davis completed another transformation in 1986 with the release of *Tutu*. It included synthesisers, drum loops and samples. The album was met with critical acclaim.

He died of pneumonia in California in 1991.

INSIGHTS FOR INNOVATORS

You cannot please everyone, so do not try. Innovation means breaking with convention and that will upset many people. Davis constantly sought to try new forms of musical expression. Often, this was initially unpopular with his fans.

Try fusion. Mix what you know with something new and different. Many inventions are fresh combinations of existing products or ideas. What is new is the way that two concepts are combined. Gutenberg fused a coin punch with a wine press, Henry Ford fused an assembly line with car construction, Miles Davis fused jazz and rock.

Never be satisfied with what you have already achieved. Miles Davis had a constantly restless approach to jazz. He courted controversy as he strove to try the new. He led significant developments in jazz across five decades. Great innovators do not rest on their laurels – they continue to innovate.

PABLO PICASSO

(1881 – 1973)

The most famous painter of the modern era

The creative genius of the Spanish artist, Pablo Picasso, changed art completely. For Picasso, what he saw with his eyes was only the starting point for his imagination to portray the image in radical ways.

Picasso was born in Malaga in Spain and studied art in Barcelona and Madrid. In 1903, he moved to Paris to start his own studio and, subsequently, he spent most of his life in France. Initially, he was a conventional artist who painted realistic pictures. But he soon developed his own distinctive style and continued to experiment. In 1901, he entered what is known as his 'Blue Period'. Feeling lonely and depressed over the death of a close friend, he painted pictures of poverty, desperation and anguish, almost exclusively in shades of blue and green. Subsequently, he fell in love and gained a financial backer, his mood improved and he entered his 'Rose Period' in 1904.

In 1907, Picasso broke the mould. He produced a painting unlike anything that anyone had ever painted before. *Les Demoiselles d'Avignon* was a startling abstract portrayal of five nude prostitutes. They were distorted with angular geometric shapes and sharp blotches of blues, greens and greys. This one painting changed the direction of art. It was the start of Cubism, an artistic style pioneered by Picasso and his friend and fellow painter, Georges Braque. Cubism was a destructive and creative movement in which the artist does not paint realistic or recognisable images, but uses shapes, such as cubes and triangles, to break apart and reconstruct a subject from several viewpoints simultaneously.

His styles continued to change and burst into new forms. He became a leader in the Surrealist movement. He used colours and shapes not to please audiences but to shock and disturb them. His famous painting *Guernica*, in 1937, was a terrifying portrayal of the horrors of war. It represented the bombing of the town of Guernica in the Spanish Civil War.

Picasso was a master in many art forms. He produced drawings, lithographs, etchings, sculptures, pottery, ceramics and stage designs. He continued to work and produce art prolifically until his death in Mougins in France in 1973.

Picasso is, unquestionably, the most celebrated, revolutionary and influential painter of the twentieth century. He reinvented himself continually with radically different styles, so much so that some critics consider him to be five separate artists rather than one.

INSIGHTS FOR INNOVATORS

Master the current methods and then replace them with something extraordinary. Picasso was an excellent classical painter but, after he had mastered the skill, he eschewed convention and developed his own methods. Not once, but several times.

Believe in your own genius and apply it prolifically and in different media. Picasso said, 'Whenever I wanted to say something, I said it the way I believed I should. Different themes inevitably require different methods of expression. This does not imply either evolution or progress; it is a matter of following the idea one wants to express and the way in which one wants to express it.'

DID YOU KNOW ?... Picasso rarely paid a bill. His signature was so valuable to collectors that a cheque bearing it was kept often for its value rather than cashed. If he took his friends to a restaurant, he would pay sometimes simply by signing the bill.

R oy Lichtenstein was a mainstream abstract painter in the 1950s. His art was admired and sold modestly well. He was seen as a competent run-of-the-mill artist whose abstract paintings were standard fare. One day, his young son showed him a cartoon of Mickey Mouse in a comic book and said, 'I bet you can't paint anything as good as that, Dad.' Lichtenstein took on the challenge and started making large garish paintings that looked like comic-book cartoons. His friends, critics and art lovers were aghast. It was a complete rejection of conventional abstract art. They accused him of selling out with his cheap and childish images. They said it was trashy commercialism. Lichtenstein realised that, for the first time in his life, his art was provoking a vigorous reaction. He decided that he preferred to be notorious rather than anonymous. He carried on making bigger and bolder pictures. Critics panned his work as vulgar and empty. The title of a *Life* magazine article in 1964 asked, 'Is He the Worst Artist in the U.S.?' But Lichtenstein endured the criticism and went on to become a leading figure in the Pop Art Movement. Eventually, his work became popular. The critics who had savaged his early exhibitions now showered praise on him. He had created a style all his own.

Roy Fox Lichtenstein was born in 1923, in New York City. Growing up in Manhattan, the boy showed a keen interest in science and comic books. He was drafted into the army during the Second World War and served in Europe. After the war, he studied art and, in 1949, he gained a Master of Fine Arts degree from Ohio State University.

As a leading figure in the Pop Art Movement, alongside Andy Warhol and Jasper Johns, he elevated the comic strip into high art. He was influenced heavily by popular advertising and comic books while using parody for his inspiration. He never took himself too seriously nor claimed to be a great artist. In 2015, 18 years after his death, his painting *Nurse* was sold at auction for $95 million.

INSIGHTS FOR INNOVATORS

It is more important to be different than to be better. It is no good launching a 'me too' product that is similar to, or even slightly better than, most other products on the market. Lichtenstein was just another good artist who went unnoticed until he deliberately did something different and radical.

A strong reaction, even a strong negative reaction, is better than no reaction. Do not be afraid of upsetting people. Lichtenstein's paintings were purposefully controversial. Bland products upset no one, but delight no one, and they get lost in the welter of goods on offer. If your contentious new offering is popular with a small segment of the market, then you can focus on pleasing and then growing a loyal fanbase.

Take inspiration from children. It was his child's comments that led Lichtenstein to change his style. A child's view of the world is uncomplicated and direct. It can help focus your thinking in a fundamental way.

SALVADOR DALI

(1904 – 1989)

Spanish Surrealist painter

I n January 1952, the renowned artist Salvador Dali appeared on the US TV game show *What's My Line?* You can see the remarkable video on YouTube. The panel members were blindfolded and had to question the guest to determine his identity. Almost every question they asked, he answered in the affirmative. 'Are you a performer?' 'Yes.' 'Are you a writer?' 'Yes.' 'Are you an artist?' 'Yes.' And so on, until one panellist said, in frustration, 'There is nothing this man does not do!'

Dali, born in 1904 in Spain, was most famous as an artist and as the outstanding exponent of the Surrealist movement. His most celebrated painting is entitled *The Persistence of Memory*; it features images of soft, melting pocket watches. But he was also an architect; he designed the museum in his home town of Figueres. He was a sculptor and furniture maker – his most famous pieces were the *Lobster Telephone* and the *Mae West Lips Sofa*. He was a jeweller making many intricate pieces of jewellery – some with moving parts. He was very active in theatre and film, constructing sets. He collaborated with Alfred Hitchcock to create the dream sequence in *Spellbound*. He wrote novels and his non-fiction works included the revealing titles *The Secret Life of Salvador Dalí* (1942) and *Diary of a Genius* (1952–63). He worked with photography, textiles and fashion. In short, he was a master of all trades.

Dali had great self-belief to the extent that he was an egotist who was desperate for attention. He grew a flamboyant moustache that became his trademark. He was a shameless publicity seeker and was, perhaps, the first great artist to mount serious PR campaigns on his own behalf. He was deliberately provocative and shocking and this increased his media coverage. His various antics were seen as gimmicks by his critics but as performance art by his fans.

Dali died in 1989. He has since become revered as a major inspiration by many modern artists, such as Damien Hirst and

Jeff Koons. His image is a worldwide cultural icon for everything fantastic and surreal.

INSIGHTS FOR INNOVATORS

Try other mediums. Dali wanted to flaunt his genius himself in every art form he could find. Not all of Dali's experiments succeeded but enough did for his reputation to grow to towering proportions. He applied his brilliance and creativity without fear, wherever he could. Express yourself in more than one medium, if you can do it well. It should increase your exposure and chance of success.

Be your own PR specialist. Dali used deliberate shock and gaudy ostentation to generate publicity for his work. He revelled in the attention of fans and the media. You do not need to be such a flamboyant egotist, but you should still invest in publicising your work and innovations. No false modesty, please.

DID YOU KNOW?... Salvador Dali had an older brother who was also named Salvador Dali. He was born in 1901 and died of gastroenteritis in 1903. The following year, the Dalis had the son who went on to be the great artist. Perhaps this strange circumstance contributed to the painter's surreal view of life.

WOODY ALLEN

(BORN 1935)

Comedian, actor, film director

Talking about his film *To Rome with Love*, Woody Allen said, 'I've got great people, and they make me look good. That's the thing; you hire Penelope Cruz, Ellen Page or Alec Baldwin and they're great. They were great before they met me, they'll be great after they leave me. And I exploit them. I look like a hero, but you know, that's the trick.' In this quote, Allen reveals a secret shared by successful managers, directors and leaders – hire really excellent people and then exploit them.

Heywood 'Woody' Allen was born in Brooklyn, New York, in 1935. He is a comedian, film director, screenwriter, actor and author. He is celebrated for his romantic comedy films, which involve pathos, parody and slapstick. His career has spanned more than six decades.

Allen studied at New York University in 1953, but failed a course in motion picture production. After leaving university, he started work as a comedy writer. He wrote scripts and jokes for TV shows. He performed as a stand-up comedian on the New York comedy circuit, developing his own unique style of insecure, intellectual, self-deprecating Jewish humour.

In the1960s, Allen wrote and directed films, initially witty comedies and then serious drama. Often, he appeared in his films, sometimes as a star and sometimes in a minor role. He directed over 40 films, including *Annie Hall* (1977), *Manhattan* (1979), *Hannah and Her Sisters* (1986) and *Match Point* (2005). He has won four Academy Awards: three for Best Original Screenplay and one for Best Director (*Annie Hall*).

Allen is also a talented musician and he performs regularly as a jazz clarinettist at small venues in New York.

INSIGHTS FOR INNOVATORS

Innovate by recruiting people who are smarter than you are. Give them clear goals and then get out of their way. Give them plenty of freedom to develop their own ideas. Work them hard. Give them responsibility. This means that you can do less of the everyday stuff because they will cover it for you. You can then spend more time on high-level strategic and interesting issues. Maintain a light-touch supervision just to check that they are broadly on the right track.

Do not tell your people what to do. Woody Allen tells his stars what the goals are and then asks for their ideas and suggestions. Very often, their best ideas are better than yours. So, go with their ideas. Let them implement their own suggestions – they will work twice as hard to prove they were right. Of course, you give them the praise and credit for the innovations, but it makes you and your department look really good.

PART 2
BUSINESS LEADER

Akio Morita was born in Nagoya, Japan in 1921. His father owned a business brewing sake. It had been in the family for 14 generations and it was expected that Akio, the oldest son, would step into the business, but the boy was more interested in electronics than in brewing.

Morita studied Physics at Osaka Imperial University and served as a naval lieutenant during the Second World War. While in the Japanese Navy he met an electrical engineer, Masru Ibuka, and, in 1946, the two men decided to form a business together. They founded Tokyo Telecommunications Engineering Corporation and their first product was an automatic rice cooker, which failed to sell well. There was little consumer demand in a society impoverished by the war, so Morita decided to focus on export markets. At that time, Japanese companies had a reputation for producing cheap, low-quality products that often were copies of Western merchandise. Morita and his partner wanted to break away from this approach and offer high-quality, innovative electronic goods.

In 1950, they developed Japan's first magnetic tape recorder. It was their first real success. Five years later, Morita designed a pocket-sized transistor radio for the American market, but it was just a little too large to fit in a shirt pocket. Morita came up with an innovative marketing idea. He gave all his salesmen shirts with larger pockets so that, during demonstrations, they could slip the radio in and out of their pockets. This became the first commercially successful transistor radio and sold well around the world.

Morita grasped the importance of brands and saw that the name Tokyo Telecommunications Engineering Corp. was an impediment to success. All his colleagues in Japan liked it, but he wanted to find something easily memorable in global markets. In 1958, he changed the company name to Sony because it was short and friendly. In 1960, he founded Sony

Corporation of America and, in 1961, it became the first Japanese company listed on the New York Stock Exchange.

In the 1970s, portable tape players became popular for serious recording, but Morita thought that most products were big and unwieldy. He wanted to create a small battery-powered tape player for the consumer market. He designed a cassette product with headphones instead of speakers and with no record function – just playback. Most experts, including those at Sony, thought that a tape recorder that could not record was a ridiculous idea. But Morita was convinced that he could make something so portable and convenient that people would want it. In 1979, he created the Sony Walkman that went on to be the most successful personal electronics product ever with sales of over 250 million units. It changed the way that people listened to music.

Under Morita, Sony set new standards in product innovation. The company introduced the first commercial battery-powered portable TV, the first colour home video recorder, the 3 ½ inch floppy drive, 8 mm video tape and the audio CD in a joint effort with Phillips. Sony set a new standard in TV picture quality with the Trinitron tube. In the 1980s, Sony extended the Walkman brand with the launch of the Discman portable CD player.

Akio Morita was not only a brilliant engineer; he was also a shrewd businessman, a creative marketer and a people person. He was naturally friendly and outgoing. He was able to understand Western consumers and to bridge the communication gap between Japan and the West.

Ibuka left Sony in 1976. Morita stepped down from the company in 1994. He died of pneumonia in 1999, at the age of 78. At the time of his death, Akio Morita was the most famous Japanese citizen in the world and Sony was the leading electronics consumer brand in the USA.

INSIGHTS FOR INNOVATORS

Try innovation by elimination. Morita took the traditional tape recorder and eliminated speakers and the record function. He made something simpler, smaller, cheaper and easier to use. What can you eliminate from your product or service to make it simpler for users?

Ignore the doubters. Many people doubted the concept of the Walkman, but Morita persisted and proved them wrong. Most commentators thought that transistor radios could not compete with traditional valve radios because valve radios offered higher quality. But Sony transistor radios were lighter and cheaper. Their quality improved over time and they came to dominate the market.

Ignore focus groups and, instead, anticipate customers' needs. There was no market research indicating a need for a Walkman-type product. In a similar fashion to Steve Jobs, Morita trusted his judgement and intuition more than input from focus groups. Routine marketers analyse current needs of customers. True innovators anticipate the future needs of customers.

DID YOU KNOW?... The name Sony was chosen by Morita and Ibuka for two reasons: s*onus* is the Latin word for sound (and gives us sonic); 'Sonny Boy' was an Americanism used in Japan to mean a clever young man.

ANNE MULCAHY

(BORN 1952)

Former chairperson and CEO at Xerox Corporation

When Anne Mulcahy was appointed CEO of Xerox Corp. in 2001, many people were surprised, including Mulcahy herself. She had never run a company before and had little financial experience, having worked mainly in sales and human resources functions. Xerox faced huge financial problems and the stock price fell 15 per cent on news of her appointment. The stock market had little confidence in her ability to turn around the stumbling giant.

She took over the reins of a company that was close to bankruptcy. Xerox had made losses for the previous six years and its debts amounted to over $17 billion. Its credit rating had been slashed. Expenses were running out of control. The company was under investigation by the Securities and Exchange Commission for financial irregularities. Customers and shareholders were unhappy.

She started by talking and listening to employees and customers. She said, 'When I became CEO, I spent the first 90 days on planes travelling to various offices and listening to anyone who had a perspective on what was wrong with the company. I think if you spend as much time listening as talking, that's time well spent.'

Her advisers urged her to declare bankruptcy because of the mountain of debt. But, instead, she implemented a dramatic recovery plan. Capital spending was cut by half and general expenses by one third. But she ignored advice to cut research and development. She invested in innovation. She sold unprofitable units, eliminated 28,000 jobs and slashed administrative expenses while protecting sales and R&D. She saved the company.

During the whole painful process she placed great emphasis on communication. In order to promote her vision for the future of Xerox, she created a fictitious *Wall Street Journal* article describing Xerox in the year 2005. 'We outlined the things we hoped to accomplish as though we had already achieved them,' said

Mulcahy. 'We included performance metrics, even quotes from Wall Street analysts. It was really our vision of what we wanted the company to become.' The article was sent to every employee and people understood where the company was headed.

The company's turnaround was built on restructuring and the introduction of innovative products and services. In 2008, Mulcahy was named CEO of the Year by *Chief Executive* magazine.

Anne Mulcahy was born in 1952. She joined Xerox as a field sales representative in 1976 and rose through the ranks. In 2009, she retired from her position as CEO, having accomplished what *Money Magazine* described as 'the great turnaround story of the post-crash era'.

INSIGHTS FOR INNOVATORS

If you want to lead change, you have to communicate your vision. Mulcahy devoted time to talking to people and listening. 'Good leaders listen,' she said. She painted a different and better future for the company and communicated it with a mock-up of a future *Wall Street Journal* article. She changed the culture and processes in a huge organisation with the power of communication and with clear and decisive actions.

Believe in yourself and your people. Many pessimists thought that Xerox was finished. They urged filing for Chapter 11 bankruptcy and for a halt to spending on new product development. Mulcahy listened to them, but chose the advice of customers and employees who could see what was wrong with the company and gave her the impetus to fix it. She invested in the future and she made it happen.

DID YOU KNOW?... In the 1970s, the Xerox Palo Alto Research Centre (PARC) developed a remarkable number of ground-breaking computing technologies. These included the first mouse, bitmapped display, window-based GUI, ethernet networking, file servers, print servers and email. They could never successfully commercialise them. Steve Jobs visited PARC and was impressed. He later said, 'They just had no idea what they had.' He recruited some of the top engineers from PARC researchers to join Apple to develop their ideas.

CLARENCE BIRDSEYE

(1886 – 1956)

Creator of the frozen food industry

In 1912, a young American scientist, Clarence Birdseye, departed on a fur-trading expedition to Labrador in Canada. While he was there, he noticed that the local Eskimos kept their fish fresh in winter by freezing them in the ice. He was intrigued to find that the fish retained their flavour and did not deteriorate. He wondered whether the same process could be applied to other foodstuffs and developed on a commercial scale.

Birdseye returned to the USA and worked on this idea. He developed a 'Quick Freeze Machine', which copied the method used by the Eskimos. The machine worked for a range of foods, including fruit and vegetables. In 1924, Birdseye launched the world's first frozen-food company, the General Seafood Corporation. His surname became the brand name and trademark for his products. His key new invention was the double belt freezer that froze fish quickly as they moved on a pair of stainless steel belts. He patented this invention, which subsequently was adopted by many other companies.

In 1929, his company was bought by General Foods, which kept the Birds Eye trademark, turning it into two words. Clarence worked there as President of the Birds Eye Frosted Foods division and, over the next decade, he and his company changed the way Americans stored and cooked food.

During his lifetime, Birdseye patented more than 300 inventions, including a process for dehydrating food. He introduced refrigerated wagons so that Birds Eye could distribute frozen products all over the country.

Clarence Birdseye was born in New York in 1886, the sixth of nine children. As a boy, he had a keen interest in nature, botany and science. His parents could not afford a college education for him so he took a job as a taxidermist. He then worked as a government field naturalist for the US Biological Survey. He supplemented his income with fur trading, which led him to Canada and his great discovery. He died in 1956 by which time frozen food was a massive industry worldwide.

INSIGHTS FOR INNOVATORS

Look outside for ideas. Solve your problem by adapting a concept that works somewhere else. Birdseye would not have produced his innovation if he had stayed in New York. He saw an idea in a completely different environment, a snowy wilderness, and adapted it for widespread use in an urban environment. He knew that people in cities needed supplies of healthy, fresh food.

Be curious about how other people in different places use technology and solve problems. Curiosity and risk taking are two of the hallmarks of innovators. Birdseye said, 'I do not consider myself a remarkable person. I am just a guy with a very large bump of curiosity and a gambling instinct.'

Patent your inventions. Birdseye secured his fortune by protecting his designs with patents.

DANIEL PETER

(1836 – 1919)

The inventor of milk chocolate

What do you do when an innovation threatens to put you out of business? Daniel Peter, who was born in 1836, was a Swiss man who ran a candlestick-making business with his brother Julien in Vevey, Switzerland. In the early nineteenth century, candles were the primary source of lighting at night, so business was good.

In 1859, Colonel Drake of Pennsylvania had discovered oil and that led to the development of kerosene and kerosene lamps. These were introduced to Switzerland in the mid-1860s and their popularity caused a significant drop in the demand for candles.

The Peter brothers had a problem. They had a factory that could pour liquid candle wax into moulds, but demand for candles was falling. Julien decided to stay in the candle business, but Daniel wanted to use some of the equipment and his skills in a different endeavour. He decided to pour chocolate instead of wax. He studied chocolate making and started his own business.

At that time, chocolate was dark and bitter. Daniel Peter tried to develop a softer chocolate by adding milk, but he found great difficulty in removing the water from the milk. His experiments ended with mildew forming on the chocolate or with a rancid product. Eventually, he heard of a neighbour in the same town who had developed a condensed milk as a baby food. That man's name was Henri Nestlé. Using condensed milk, together they were able to perfect a method for the manufacture of milk chocolate. In 1887, after many unsuccessful experiments, Daniel Peter developed the original formula for what was to become the first successful milk chocolate in the world. He called his product Gala after the Greek word meaning 'from the milk'. In 1879, the pair formed the Nestlé Company. Their new product proved immensely popular around the world.

In 1896, Daniel Peter formed the association of Swiss Chocolatiers and, in 1904, several companies merged under the name of the Nestlé brand.

Daniel Peter continued to work in the Nestlé factory until his death in 1919.

INSIGHTS FOR INNOVATORS

Innovations destroy, even as they create. When innovation threatens your business, you must adapt or die. The threat of the destruction of his candle-making business was the spur for Daniel Peter to look for new ventures. What innovations or trends threaten your business today and what can you do about it?

Transfer your current skills to a new environment and open up new opportunities. Daniel Peter's skill was in moulding liquids. He transferred this from candles to chocolate.

With whom can you collaborate who has the skills that you lack? By cooperating with Henri Nestlé, Daniel Peter was able to co-create a product that changed the flavour of chocolate around the world. Maybe you can find someone locally, as Daniel Peter did.

INGVAR KAMPRAD

(BORN 1926)

Founder of IKEA

Ingvar Feodor Kamprad was born in 1926 on a small farm in the Swedish province of Småland. He had an austere upbringing and the lessons he learnt in frugality stayed with him thoughout his life.

At the age of six, the boy started a business selling matches to neighbours. He bought the matches in bulk and sold them in small inexpensive packs. He went on to sell seeds, pens, pencils and even fish in this way. In 1943, he founded IKEA using his initials and those of Elmtaryd Agunnaryd, his childhood home.

In 1947, he began buying and reselling furniture but, by the mid-1950s, his local suppliers complained that he was selling their goods too cheaply, so he decided to design and make his own products. Kamprad came up with a new concept. He took apart assembled furniture and developed flat pack kits from which customers could assemble their furniture. They were simple and affordable for customers. The packs took less space than regular furniture, so they saved IKEA money in transport and storage. Kamprad believed that everyone should be able to afford stylish modern furniture and that IKEA could meet this need.

The business grew, expanding first across Scandinavia and then the world. At the IKEA opening in Shanghai, there were 80,000 people keen to visit the store. In 2016, IKEA could boast over 370 stores with over 880 million visitors a year in total. Kamprad achieved this growth without ever borrowing money or issuing stock.

Kamprad has become one of the richest men in the world, yet he retains and embodies a frugal approach. At the age of 85, he still travels the world to visit IKEA stores. He drives an old Volvo car, stays in cheap hotels and flies economy class. He addresses IKEA employees as coworkers and encourages everyone to dress informally, enjoy work, give excellent service and keep costs down.

INSIGHTS FOR INNOVATORS

Innovate the process by transferring some of the job to the customer. Clients in IKEA stores act as warehousemen when they collect their goods and they act as furniture assemblers when they put their flat packs together. This saves costs, but the customers do not complain. They enjoy the competitive prices and the challenge of assembling the units.

Practise frugal innovation. Most innovators have limited resources, so it is important not to waste them. Kamprad has set an example all his life of keeping costs down, keeping prices down, minimising waste and maximising customer satisfaction.

Retain a distinctive culture. Although IKEA is a global brand, it has a very Scandinavian culture and atmosphere. For example, the same product names are used worldwide. Beds have Norwegian place names, sofas have Swedish place names, tables have Finnish place names, whilst chairs and rugs have Danish names.

DID YOU KNOW?... Every IKEA store has a play area for small children. It is called Småland, the name of the Swedish province where Kamprad was born, meaning small land in Swedish. Parents can stay in touch with their children through mobile devices.

JEFF BEZOS

(BORN 1964)

Entrepreneur and founder of Amazon.com

As a boy brought up in Florida, Jeff Bezos developed a keen interest in computers. He graduated from Princeton in 1986 with a degree in Computer Science and Electrical Engineering. He then worked for an investment firm in New York before quitting his well-paid position in 1994 to start Amazon, just as internet commerce was beginning to take off. He started the company in his garage where he wrote the software systems for online commerce. He opened his virtual bookstore in 1995. The success of the company was spectacular. Within two months of opening, sales were running at $20,000 a week and they continued to escalate.

Amazon.com went public in 1997. Traditional bookstores responded with their own websites, but none was as appealing, as agile or as successful as Amazon. Bezos diversified his product range first with CDs and videos, followed by electronic goods, toys and clothes. Sales leapt from half a million dollars in 1995 to $17 billion in 2011.

Amazon pioneered many innovative practices, such as recommending what customers would like based on an algorithm that compared previous buying patterns with those of other consumers. Although its sales of new books were growing very healthily, in 2002 Amazon introduced a service whereby people could sell second-hand books through the company's website. This was surprising, as it appeared that each second-hand book sale meant the loss of a larger-margin new book sale. The move was controversial and Bezos sent out an open letter explaining Amazon's actions. In it, he argued that selling second-hand books was good for customers and, therefore, good for the industry.

Amazon developed tremendous IT skills and capacity as it grew, rapidly selling books and other products online. It was a giant in B to C (business to consumer) products. After the dot. com crash in 2000, Amazon found itself with excess IT capacity in its data centres. It offered web services to businesses and became a leader in B to B (business to business) services – a completely different field from its original strength. By 2015, Amazon Web Services was the world's leading provider of Cloud infrastructure services.

Bezos realised that there was a potential customer need for an inexpensive reader for electronic books. But Amazon had no experience or competence in electronic product design or manufacture. Amazon's strengths lay in excellent web services, software and logistics. For the company to launch its own hardware product would be a major step into unknown territory. Yet that is what they did in 2007 with the launch of the Kindle. It became a tremendous success.

The company continued to experiment and innovate in a remarkable number of fields. It produced its own TV and film features. In 2013, it announced plans for drone deliveries. Not all the innovations succeeded. In 2014, Amazon entered the smartphone market with the release of the Fire Phone. It was considered to be too gimmicky and it flopped.

Bezos has a diverse range of business interests. He founded an aerospace company, Blue Origin, to provide private space flights. In 2013, he purchased *The Washington Post* newspaper. In 2016, his personal wealth was estimated to be some $60 billion, making him one of the five richest people in the USA.

INSIGHTS FOR INNOVATORS

Disrupt your own business before someone else does. Offering second-hand books at low margin threatened Amazon's higher value new book sales, but this did not bother Bezos. He wanted to own that segment of the market too and to prevent a competitor from seizing it.

Innovate in another field with your spare capacity. Bezos led Amazon on a remarkable pivot. Because of its internal IT expertise and spare server capacity, the company became a leader in web services for businesses – a completely different field from its core business in consumer goods delivery. Do you have unused capacity that can be put to an innovative use?

Anticipate customer needs. Amazon was selling conventional books, but Bezos could see that some people would want to read electronic books on computers. He stole a march on competitors by developing Amazon's proprietary e-book reader, the Kindle. It was attractively priced and scooped the market. For a bookseller to build a consumer electronics product device was a risky venture, but it paid off. What things will people want to do differently in the future?

LEVI STRAUSS

(1829 – 1902)

Founder of an iconic fashion item –
the blue jean

Levi Strauss was born in Buttenheim, Germany, in 1829 to an Ashkenazi Jewish family that suffered religious persecution. Strauss's father died when he was 16 and, two years later, he, his mother and two sisters emigrated to the USA. Initially, they lived in New York.

The California Gold Rush of 1849 caused a stampede of people seeking their fortune in the West. Strauss joined them. He went to San Francisco to sell goods to the booming mining trade. He sold clothing, fabric and other items to small shops in the region. The story goes that Strauss bought a large stock of tents to sell to miners in the gold rush, but the weather was so mild that sales of tents were poor. Strauss took a pair of scissors and cut up the heavy canvas tent material in order to make trousers for the miners to wear.

His clothing was selling well when, in 1872, a customer for the material, Jacob Davis, approached Strauss with a proposition. Davis was a tailor who had discovered a way to make the trousers last longer. He used metal rivets to reinforce the seams at certain points on the pockets and on the front fly. Davis asked Strauss to pay the fee for a patent for the process.

The patent was granted to Strauss and Davis the next year. Initially, Strauss called the strong trousers 'waist overalls', but they soon became known as blue jeans. It is claimed that they were dyed blue, as this colour hid many stains.

As the business boomed, Strauss became a great philanthropist, contributing to many local charities in San Francisco. He provided funds for 28 scholarships at the University of California at Berkeley. He died in 1902 at the age of 73. He had no children, but handed the business over to his four nephews.

Levi Strauss had launched a long-lived clothing empire. His durable and popular blue jeans became a symbol of the American West. The company he founded continues to operate to this day.

INSIGHTS FOR
INNOVATORS

When one line of approach fails, try another. Use a setback as a spur to innovation. Strauss did not persist in pushing tents when there was little demand. He adapted and used the tenting material to make trousers. He produced what his customers needed.

Collaborate to innovate. Strauss was fortunate to be approached by Jacob Davis, but he had already established a reputation as a fair man with whom to do business. He seized the opportunity and, together, he and Davis exploited the patent for riveted clothing.

DID YOU KNOW?... For many years, sales of jeans were confined mostly to working men, such as cowboys, construction workers and lumberjacks in the west of the USA. During the Second World War, blue jeans were declared an essential commodity and were sold only to people engaged in defence work. This restriction made them much more sought after. Is there a clever way to make your product more exclusive and desirable?

RAY KROC

(1902 – 1984)

The entrepreneur who built McDonald's into the world's most successful fast food chain

R ay Albert Kroc was born to parents of Czech origin in Illinois in 1902. He served as a Red Cross ambulance driver in the First World War, lying about his age to begin serving at 15. After the war, Kroc tried his hand at various careers. Over the next 30 years, he was a pianist, radio DJ, a salesman and he worked in hotels and restaurants. Eventually, Kroc became a travelling milkshake machine salesman. It was in this role that, in 1954, he came across the McDonald brothers, clients of his who had a number of restaurants in San Bernardino, California. He saw great potential in the chain and in their assembly line approach to the preparation of hamburgers. Unlike other hamburger restaurants, they offered a limited menu of choices, which meant they could focus on quick service and quality. Kroc joined them as a franchising agent for a percentage of the profits. At the time, large geographic franchises were standard industry practice, but Kroc innovated by insisting on single-store franchises in order to maintain control. He became president of McDonald's Corporation in 1955 and bought the brothers out in 1961 for $2.7 million.

Kroc introduced many efficiencies and innovations. His most important new idea was the assembly line method in order to automate and standardise the fast food process. He carefully screened applicants for franchises, searching for drive and ambition. Those chosen attended 'Hamburger University' in Elk Grove, Illinois, a first in the restaurant business, where they learnt all the techniques and methods to produce perfect hamburgers and French fries. They learnt Kroc's strict guidelines regarding preparation, portion sizes, cooking processes, cleanliness and staff management. This ensured that McDonald's food looked and tasted the same across the world. He introduced a rule that customers would get a refund automatically, if their food took more than five minutes to arrive.

In later life, Kroc became a philanthropist. He was a major donor to schools and charities and his foundation supported research and treatment of alcoholism, diabetes and other diseases.

At the time of Kroc's death in 1984, at the age of 81, McDonald's had 7,500 restaurants in 31 countries and was valued at $8 billion.

INSIGHTS FOR INNOVATORS

You need ego and tremendous self-belief. Ray Kroc said, 'To be an entrepreneur, you have to have a large ego, enormous pride and an ability to inspire others to follow your lead.' All successful pioneers have great self-belief. This gives them the strength to persevere through the bad times and the doubters.

You are never too old to start innovating. Kroc joined McDonald's as an employee at the age of 52 and became the owner of the chain at 59. He continued working in the business for the next 20 years.

Focus on the process, not just the product. Kroc's major innovations were in the systems and methods used in fast food production. The hamburgers and fries that McDonald's produced were not, necessarily, better than those of competitors. However, consistency, faster speed of service and lower costs gave the chain a winning competitive advantage. What innovations can you introduce to the systems and processes in your business? How can you streamline them and speed them up?

RICARDO SEMLER

(BORN 1959)

Brazilian industrialist

In Brazil, where traditional command and control management practices and paternalism were rife, Ricardo Semler became a legend as an industrialist who developed revolutionary ideas about how to manage people. He did just about everything differently. Most of the 3,000 workers at his manufacturing company, Semco, set their own working hours, productivity targets and schedules. The workers take majority votes on important corporate decisions. They have complete access to the company's accounts and trading data. Many set their own salaries and bonuses.

The results have been impressive. Revenues grew from $4 million in 1982 to $212 million in 2003. Semler's radical approaches to management and human relations have drawn interest and admiration from around the world. *The Wall Street Journal*'s Latin American magazine named him Latin American businessman of the year in 1990 and he was named Brazilian businessman of the year in 1990 and 1992. His book *Turning Your Own Table* became the best-selling non-fiction book in the history of Brazil.

Semler was born in 1959 in Sao Paulo. He joined his father, Antonio, in his business in the late 1970s when it was a struggling supplier to the shipbuilders. Father and son disagreed on many aspects of the business, including its strategic direction and the autocratic style of management that Antonio employed. The power struggle was resolved in 1980 when the 21-year-old Ricardo took over the company. On his first day as CEO, he fired over half of the senior managers. The company was underfinanced and could grow only very slowly. In 1990, the Brazilian economy suffered a severe slump and Semco, like many other local companies, faced ruin. Semler agreed a new deal with his workers that involved wage cuts. Employees were given the right to approve all expenditures. This revolution gave workers a full understanding of the business operations and resulted in many suggestions for improvements. Inventories were reduced by over 60 per cent while quality and delivery performance improved. Semco's fortunes recovered. The company diversified into the manufacture of sophisticated products, such as marine pumps, digital scanners, commercial dishwashers and mixing equipment.

Semler explained his approach to employee democracy, 'We insist on making important decisions collegially, and certain decisions are made by a company-wide vote. Several years ago, we needed a bigger plant for our marine division, which makes pumps, compressors and ship propellers. Real estate agents looked for months and found nothing. So we asked the employees themselves to help and, over the first weekend, they found three factories for sale, all of them nearby. We closed up shop for a day, piled everyone into buses and drove out to inspect the three buildings. Then the workers voted – and they chose a plant the counsellors didn't really want. It was an interesting situation – one that tested our commitment to participatory management. We bought the building and moved in. The workers designed the layout for a flexible manufacturing system, and they hired one of Brazil's foremost artists to paint the whole thing, inside and out, including the machinery. That plant really belongs to its employees. I feel like a guest every time I walk in.'

INSIGHTS FOR INNOVATORS

Trust your people. Semler shares all important company information with all employees. He can trust them with confidential data because he has built trust over the years and he knows that this data helps small autonomous units make better decisions.

Sweep away the bureaucracy. As Semler puts it, Semco is a company managed without managers. He eliminated most layers of management and put in place 'coordinators'. They do not hire or promote people until they have been interviewed and accepted by all their future subordinates.

Get active feedback. Twice a year, Semco subordinates evaluate managers and everybody completes a survey on company credibility and top management competence. One of the questions asked is, 'What would it take to make you quit or go on strike?'

ROB McEWEN

(BORN 1950)

Canadian businessman and mine owner

In 1990, the industrialist Rob McEwen took over an old and underperforming gold mine with a land area of 55,000 acres in Ontario, Canada. The Red Lake mine had various problems. Gold production was falling and costs were rising. McEwen was convinced that the mine could produce more gold but he did not know how. Then, in 1999, he went to a seminar on computing at MIT. He learnt about the open source operating system, Linux, in which the code is visible to all and anyone can make suggestions for improvements. This triggered a remarkable idea.

In 2000, he launched the Goldcorp Challenge. He published all the data on the mine online for geologists and engineers from anywhere in the world in a contest to see who could predict accurately where to mine for gold. He offered half a million Canadian dollars in prizes.

Mining experts, both within his company and outside, were appalled at the idea of exposing the mine's proprietary data to the world. The tradition in the mining industry is to be secretive about reserves and geological data. What's more, the information could have exposed the company to a hostile takeover bid.

More than 1,400 scientists, data analysts and geologists from 50 countries entered the contest and downloaded the mine's data. The creativity and accuracy of the best entries were remarkable. The winning entry was submitted by a collaboration of two Australian firms who used fractal graphics to develop a 3D picture of the mine.

McEwen was delighted, saying later, 'We drilled four of the winners' top five targets and have hit on all four.' He went on, 'From a remote site, the winners were able to analyse a database and generate targets without ever visiting the property.'

McEwen went on to transform Goldcorp from a collection of small companies into a mining giant. Its share price increased at a 30 per cent compound annual growth rate. Its market capitalisation grew from $50 million in 1993 to over $20 billion in 2015, making it the largest gold producer in the world.

INSIGHTS FOR INNOVATORS

Take an idea from a completely different field and adapt it to yours. McEwen went to a computing conference and then had the insight to adapt the concept of open source software to a gold mine. He created one of the first and most successful internet-based crowdsourcing contests.

Think like an outsider. McEwen had an advantage over his conventional mining competitors. He was not a miner. He had worked for Merrill Lynch in the investment business. He was not constrained by traditional rules and thinking. If you cannot be an outsider, then force yourself to think like an outsider.

Throw down a challenge. If you have a tough challenge, try posing it as a problem on a crowdsourcing site, such as Innocentive, Nine Sigma or Top Coder. You can harness the creative brains of solvers from all around the world.

SIDNEY BERNSTEIN

(1899 – 1993)

UK media mogul

U ntil 1954, there was only one television channel in the UK. It was the publicly owned BBC. In that year, the Government auctioned licences for commercial TV stations. These would be regional operations that could offer advertising on TV for the first time. Various companies were interested in this opportunity and, naturally, they focused on the regions with the best demographics – it seemed natural that rich regions would generate more advertising revenue. Sidney Bernstein was the managing director of a cinema chain in the south of England. He wanted to bid for a region, but he decided not to bid for the richest region. Instead, he bid for the wettest region in the UK, the north-west of England. He was successful and he established Granada Television, based in Manchester, serving the north of England.

He surmised that, if it was sunny outside, people might be in their gardens or go for a walk. If it was pouring down with rain, they were more likely to stay inside and watch television.

Bernstein was born into a large Jewish immigrant family who lived just outside London. His father was Swedish and his mother was Russian. Bernstein left school at 15 to work in his father's cinema theatre business. At the age of 22, he took over the business, which had just four theatres. He was always adventurous and innovative. In 1930, he opened a super-cinema, seating over 1,000 people. Bernstein employed a Russian theatre designer to create opulent interiors for his cinemas with Gothic, Renaissance and Moorish influences. He was a pioneer in undertaking market research into the tastes and habits of cinema audiences. He launched Saturday morning shows for children.

Although a wealthy businessman, Bernstein was an active left-wing politician and anti-fascist. He served six years as a Labour local government councillor. During the Second World War, he was an adviser to the Ministry of Information and produced anti-Nazi films that influenced pro-British sentiment in the USA. Subsequently, he brought his friend Alfred Hitchcock back from Hollywood and produced some of his films in the UK.

Granada Television established a strong reputation for innovative high-quality drama and documentary shows. In 1957, Granada produced the top 10 programmes by ratings in its region. In 1962, it was the first television outlet to screen the Beatles on British television. Over the next 20 years, the company successfully diversified into television rental, publishing, bingo, bowling alleys and motorway service areas.

Sidney Bernstein retired from Granada in 1979 and died in 1993.

INSIGHTS FOR INNOVATORS

When everyone else is facing in one direction, deliberately look in another direction. The other companies bidding for franchises were asking, 'Which is the wealthiest region?' Bernstein asked, 'Which is the wettest region?' This is just like David Bowie's song 'Changes', in which he sings about turning and facing the strange. This is what Bernstein did.

Popular does not have to mean low-quality. Granada Television pioneered some legendary new TV series, including *Coronation Street*, *World in Action* and *What the Papers Say*. Bernstein took a strong personal interest in each of the shows and insisted on high standards of content and production quality. Commentators of the day feared that commercial television stations would pander to the lowest tastes and cheapest shows, but Bernstein confounded them.

SIR CHARLES DUNSTONE

(BORN 1964)

Cell phone entrepreneur

S ir Charles Dunstone is the chairman and cofounder of Carphone Warehouse (CPW), a UK company that now claims to be the world's largest mobile phone retailer.

During the 1980s, Dunstone worked as a salesman at NEC, promoting mobile phones. In those days, cell phones were large, awkward and expensive. They were sold in corporate contracts mainly to large corporations. Dunstone foresaw a big growth in the business – particularly for small businesses and individual users who, until then, were poorly served.

He decided to gamble his life savings of £6,000 on the opportunity. In 1989, at the age of 25, he set up his own business selling mobile phones from his apartment in Central London. He called his company Carphone Warehouse in order to appeal to a mass market.

Growth was spectacular. When his company made its initial public offering on the London Stock Exchange in 2000, it was valued at £1.7 billion. In 2014, Carphone Warehouse merged with Dixons to form Dixons Carphone.

In 2005, Dunstone was named *The Daily Telegraph*'s Business Person of the Year. He was knighted in 2012 for services to the mobile communications industry and to charity.

In 2003, Carphone Warehouse (CPW) started selling a new model, the Razr from Motorola. Sales were doing reasonably well, but Dunstone's marketing team noted something unusual. Some 80 per cent of sales of this model were to men and only 20 per cent to women. Dunstone was interested to know why. His team investigated and reported that the phone was available only in black and silver grey – both rather masculine colours.

Dunstone called the head of Motorola's phone business in Europe and asked if it would be possible to produce the Motorola Razr in bright pink. Coloured phones were relatively rare at the time. The answer was cautious but positive. Dunstone then asked if CPW could have a worldwide exclusive on pink Razrs. The Motorola chief replied that it would be possible, but there was a minimum order of 250,000 units. Dunstone gathered his team and discussed the idea. What would they do with a quarter of a million pink phones? What if the phones were not popular? Would they be able to shift them with promotional offers and special deals? They weighed up the risks and rewards and decided that they could handle the downside. Dunstone placed the order.

The only place in the world where you could get a pink Razr was Carphone Warehouse. In the end, over 600,000 units were sold. It was a gamble that paid off.

INSIGHTS FOR INNOVATORS

Roll the dice. Innovative business leaders like Sir Charles Dunstone make careful bets. He saw a gap in the market for mobile phone services to small businesses, so he bet his savings on launching his company. He made a series of acquisitions that enabled him to take on and outmanoeuvre large incumbent European telephone companies. His company was more agile than its larger competitors.

Spot a gap in the market. Dunstone's team analysed the market and saw an opportunity for a phone that was more appealing for women. Wherever there is an unmet need, there is an opportunity for innovation.

Calculate the risks. Weigh up the options and be prepared to take a gamble, if you feel confident it is the right thing to do. Do the maths but trust your intuition. Estimate the downside risk by asking, 'What is the upside and what is the worst that can happen?' Dunstone was able to take a big risk on the pink Razr because he knew he had estimated the downside.

SOICHIRO HONDA

(1906 – 1991)

Industrialist and founder of Honda
Motor Corporation

oichiro Honda was born the son of a blacksmith in a small village in Japan in 1906. As a little boy, he was thrilled by the sight of the first car he ever saw. In later life, he declared that he never forgot the smell of oil it gave off. Thus began his lifelong fascination with motors. He left school at 16 with little educational achievement and became an apprentice auto repairman. At the age of 22, he started his own motor repair business.

He took part in auto races. His company started making piston rings for Toyota. In the mid-1940s, he designed and built a small engine that could be attached to a bicycle to create an economical low-powered motorbike. It was a big success in post-war Japan and, in 1948, he founded the Honda Motor Company. This became the largest motorbike company in Japan and, eventually, in the world.

As a successful industrialist, Soichiro Honda broke the mould of Japanese businessmen. He continued to race cars. He loved and encouraged press publicity. He studied and expressed admiration for US business methods. He promoted on merit rather than on age or family relationship, as was common practice in Japan.

In 1972, Honda introduced its new car, the Civic, to the US market. It was well-engineered but, unlike most US cars, it was small and very economical. It became popular and Honda opened manufacturing plants for cars and motorcycles in the USA. Honda was the first Japanese automobile manufacturer to release a dedicated luxury brand, the Acura, in 1986.

In his seventies, Soichiro enjoyed skiing, hang-gliding and ballooning. He was an accomplished artist and held a private pilot's licence. He died in 1991 aged 84.

INSIGHTS FOR INNOVATORS

Persevere through the failures. Honda Motor Company entered the US market in 1959 with its range of low-powered motorcycles. It endured failure after failure as it learned the hard way that little motorcycles popular in the Tokyo suburbs were not well received on the wide open roads of the USA. Honda eventually brought out a range of high-powered bikes that became very popular. Soichiro Honda said, 'Many people dream of success. Success can only be achieved through repeated failure and introspection. Success represents the 1 per cent of your work that results from the 99 per cent that is called failure.'

If you are an outsider, make the most of it. Outsiders can see things that the natives cannot. As a Japanese businessman who was extrovert, opinionated and fluent in English, Soichiro Honda became a celebrity in the US business community. He brought a cultured external view that made him popular with the media. This helped raise the profile of Honda Cars in the USA. Sometimes, it is an advantage not to be one of the locals.

ZHANG RUIMIN

(BORN 1949)

China's champion innovator

I n 1984, a young manager called Zhang Ruimin took control of a loss-making fridge factory in Qingdao, China. He was appalled at the low standards of workmanship and quality in its products. In a dramatic expression of his wrath, he gave out sledgehammers and asked factory workers to join him in smashing 76 faulty fridges in front of a large group of shocked employees. The message was clear – poor quality was no longer acceptable.

Since then, Ruimin has focused on quality, innovation and branding in order to build the company, Haier, into the largest appliance maker in the world, with a turnover of over $26 billion. One of the elements of Haier's success was learning from customers. Zhang regularly sent engineers into the marketplace to see how customers were using their products. The insights gained spurred innovation. For example, engineers learnt that in rural China some people were using Haier washing machines to wash vegetables (in particular, sweet potatoes). What did Zhang do? He told his development team to design a new cold water washing cycle specifically for vegetables. Engineers in the USA reported back that they had seen a student with two small Haier fridges set apart with a plank of wood on them that the lad had used as a desk. Haier brought out a line of fridges with a pull-out desk top. Another customer-led innovation was a freezer with a slightly less cold compartment designed to keep ice cream soft. Haier is the only Chinese company in the world's top 10 most innovative companies listing by the Boston Consulting Group.

Ruimin is recognised in China and worldwide as a great entrepreneur and innovator. Now in his sixties, he is a teetotaller who rarely takes time off and works most days in the business. His latest disruptive innovation is to jettison the company's entire middle management layer. Instead of working in separate departments, like most large corporations, Haier's 80,000 employees now work in some 2,000 fluid teams. Any employee can propose an idea and, if it is voted a winner, then that person becomes the team leader. The team manages itself and is responsible for the profit or loss of the project. The revolutionary idea of self-organising teams has been tried successfully elsewhere by companies, such as WL Gore and Oticon, but it is still seen as radical – particularly in China. Ruimin told *The Economist* he wants 'a free market in talent so the cream rises'.

When asked how he intends to strike a balance between distributed teams and central control, Ruimin replied, 'We do not need a balance. An unsteady and dynamic environment is the best way to keep everyone flexible.' He added, 'Previously, employees waited to hear from the boss, now they listen to the customer.'

INSIGHTS FOR INNOVATORS

Demonstrate your passion with actions not words. When Ruimin wanted to send a strong message about quality, he did not give a PowerPoint presentation; he attacked poor products with sledgehammers.

Observe your customers. Haier finds fresh ideas for innovations by watching customers in the field and seeing how they use the company's products. Every unusual use they employ and every difficulty they find is an opportunity for innovation. So, watch out for the hackers who adapt your product in some weird way. They might just be doing you a favour.

Do not settle for the settled. Ruimin deliberately encourages an unsteady and dynamic atmosphere in order to encourage innovation. If your team is happy, homogeneous and stable, then it is time to shake things up.

PART 3
GENIUS

LUDWIG VAN BEETHOVEN

(1770 – 1827)

Peerless composer who ushered
in the Romantic Movement in music

P ossibly the greatest composer of all time, and certainly the most revolutionary, was Ludwig van Beethoven. Before Beethoven, classical music was genteel, calm, structured according to strict rules and designed to please wealthy patrons. Beethoven introduced the Romantic Movement with music that was powerful, disturbing and passionate. He composed 9 symphonies, 5 piano concertos, 1 violin concerto, 32 piano sonatas and 16 string quartets. He also composed chamber music, an opera, choral works including the celebrated *Missasolemnis*, and songs. He pushed the boundaries of music and changed the way it was composed and listened to.

Beethoven was born in 1770 in Bonn, Germany. He was one of seven children but only he and two younger brothers survived childhood. His outstanding musical talent was obvious at a young age. His father was ambitious to exploit Ludwig as a child prodigy. The boy was a brilliant pianist and, at the age of 13, he was appointed organist of the court of Maximillian Franz, the Elector of Cologne. In 1792, he moved to Vienna where he met Mozart and Haydn, both of whom influenced the nature of his early musical compositions. He went on to develop his own kind of musical style in what is known as his heroic period. Beethoven said, 'I am not satisfied with the work I have done so far. From now on I intend to take a new way.' He composed a large number of original works on a grand scale. The first major work in his new style was the Third Symphony in E flat, known as the *Eroica*. It was longer and more ambitious than any previous symphony. It received a mixed reception at its premiere in 1805. Many listeners disliked its length or misunderstood its structure, but some recognised it as a masterpiece.

Beethoven had to battle a terrible affliction. At the age of 26, he began to lose his hearing. This was a dreadful blow for a professional musician. It caused him profound depression and he even considered suicide. He became completely deaf, but this adversity impelled him to an intense level of creativity. Beethoven's late period, from 1815 until his death in 1827, is characterised by compositions of great innovation, power and intellectual depth.

He was acknowledged as a genius during his lifetime. Twenty thousand people lined the streets at his funeral in Vienna. He was a social revolutionary who deliberately broke normal conventions. Before Beethoven's time, musicians were paid servants of rich patrons. He demanded and received high fees. He disdained authority and social rank. He stopped performing at the piano, if the audience were inattentive or chatted amongst themselves.

He supported the ideals of liberation and the French Revolution. He dedicated one symphony to Napoleon, but revoked the dedication when Napoleon declared himself Emperor. The fourth movement of his ninth and final symphony contains a choral setting of Schiller's *Ode to Joy*, an anthem to the brotherhood of humanity.

INSIGHTS FOR INNOVATORS

Let your hardship inspire your creativity. Your problems and afflictions are trivial compared with those that Beethoven faced. The onset of deafness would have sent many into a spiral of depression, but Beethoven displayed tremendous determination to overcome this setback. He used the affliction of deafness as a spur for even greater and more intense musical innovation. He transformed musical forms and defied social and artistic conventions.

▶

Copy the masters then develop your style. Many great innovators started by following others before finding their own distinctive voice. Beethoven started writing music in the style of Haydn, Mozart and the great classical composers. As he grew in experience and confidence, he expressed his own unique genius and created new forms of musical expression. Do not feel that you have to be completely different from day one – you can get there over time.

Do not play it safe. Keep faith in your own ability and talents. Believe in yourself. Beethoven had great self-belief. He could have written safe compositions to please the audiences of the day, but he knew that he was writing great music that would be recognised by posterity. When musicians complained that they found his music too difficult, he answered, 'Do not worry, this is music for the future.'

MICHELANGELO

(1475 – 1564)

Genius of painting, sculpture
and architecture

Michelangelo Buonarroti, the greatest artist of the Italian Renaissance, was born in 1475 near Florence. His father was a court magistrate. When his mother fell ill, the boy was placed with a family of stonecutters where he became skilled with the hammer and chisel. At the age of 13, Michelangelo became an apprentice to the painter Domenico Ghirlandaio. He became part of the household of Lorenzo de' Medici, the leading patron of the arts in Florence. There he came under the influence of many great artists and scholars and met influential business leaders.

He spent years learning the skills of sculpture. He also studied the human form and even dissected corpses to improve his understanding of anatomy. At the age of 24, he completed his first great masterpiece, the *Pietà* (meaning pity), showing Mary holding the body of Christ. People were amazed by the realism of the work and the detail of the muscles and veins. It stands today in St Peter's Basilica in the Vatican City.

In 1500, he was commissioned by the city of Florence to produce a sculpture representing the city. Over the next four years, he carved a huge block of marble into *David*. Standing 4.3 metres high, it formed a towering figure, displaying strength, courage and vulnerability. It was celebrated as a symbol of the liberty of Florence.

Michelangelo had established a supreme reputation as a sculptor, but he was also an accomplished painter. In 1508, Pope Julius II commissioned him to paint the ceiling of the Sistine Chapel in the Vatican. The artist was, at first, reluctant to take on the job, but the Pope was insistent. It was a massive and hugely difficult undertaking. The area was nearly 550 square metres. He would have to stand on scaffolding 20 metres above ground for long periods, painting above his head on a curved ceiling divided by spandrels into multiple sections. While he was painting the barrel ceiling up close, he had to imagine what it would look like when viewed from 20 m below.

Michelangelo devised his own system of scaffolding. He painted a series of frescoes depicting scenes from the book of Genesis. The work took four years to complete. It is a peerless masterpiece of dynamic drama and vibrant colours containing some 343 characters. Visitors gazing at the work hardly notice the spandrels because they are so well fitted into the overall composition.

When it was unveiled, the ceiling was recognised at once as a supreme work of art and it confirmed Michelangelo's status as Italy's greatest living artist.

Michelangelo continued to paint and sculpt. In his later years, he became prominent as an architect, designing many buildings and, in particular, the great church of St Peter's in Rome. He died in Rome at the age of 88 in 1564.

Unlike most artists, Michelangelo found fame and wealth during his lifetime. He was the first artist to see the publication of two biographies about him while he was alive. In the centuries since his death, his reputation has grown and he is regarded as the finest artistic genius of the Renaissance.

INSIGHTS FOR INNOVATORS

Genius is hard work. Unlike some other artists (e.g. Picasso) who could dash off pictures, Michelangelo devoted years labouring over his works. He was a prickly perfectionist who worked tirelessly to accomplish his wonderful frescoes and sculptures. At a young age, he spent years honing his skills working stone. If you can alloy great talent, hard work and relentless determination to succeed, then you have a winning combination.

▶

Constraints can aid creativity. The design of the ceiling of the Sistine represented a significant challenge to the artist. But Michelangelo incorporated the curved perspectives and the many spandrels and sections into his frescoes to create an amazing kaleidoscope effect. Sometimes, the box that you have to work with helps focus your mind.

DID YOU KNOW ?... The image on the Sistine ceiling of God in the act of Creation was painted in a single day. It shows God reaching upwards and it represents Michelangelo himself in the feat of creating the fresco.

MOZART

(1756 – 1791)

Composer, prodigy and musical genius

W olfgang Amadeus Mozart was short (no more than 5 ft 4 in.), underweight and pale. His face was pockmarked from a childhood illness. He was cheerful and extravagant, but he was known for his coarse manners and rude sense of humour. This inelegant, unrefined, pockmarked man produced some of the most elegant, refined and beautiful music ever composed. He is one of the greatest musicians of all time.

Mozart was born in Salzburg, Austria in 1756. His father Leopold was a musician and he quickly recognised a prodigious talent in the boy. Mozart started playing the harpsichord at three. At five, he composed pieces. By the time he was seven, he was a virtuoso performer on violin and harpsichord. He was taken on tour as a child star, playing in Vienna, Brussels, Paris and London. Everywhere he went, people were amazed at the miracle child.

At the age of 12, he wrote his first opera as well as two symphonies and a mass. In 1769, he was appointed concert director to the Prince Archbishop of Salzburg, but there was no salary, so he had to earn a living giving performances and teaching. In Salzburg, he composed many great works, including symphonies, operas and concertos for piano or violin. He worked continuously and could compose music flawlessly with great speed. He mastered many different musical forms, including chamber music, opera, symphony, sonata, choral works and even musical comedy.

In 1782, at the age of 26, he married Constanze Weber, a singer. Generally, they were happy, but often in debt. The impecunious composer continued to write soaring and majestic music. In the last year of his short life, he composed the opera *The Magic Flute* and his great *Requiem Mass*. He died in Vienna at the age of 35.

Although he had been a celebrity as a child performer, his genius as a composer was somewhat overlooked in his later life. He was buried with a dozen other bodies in a pauper's grave, the exact location of which is unknown. He has left a legacy of over 600 musical compositions – a remarkable achievement in such a short life. He is one of the most persistently popular of classical composers and he exerted a profound influence on the development of Western music. Beethoven was keen to meet him and composed his own early works in Mozart's influence. Joseph Haydn wrote that, 'Posterity will not see such a talent again in 100 years.'

INSIGHTS FOR INNOVATORS

If you have an outstanding talent, work hard to exploit it. Mozart was pushed by his father to display his virtuosity. He went on to perform and compose in a prolific manner throughout his life.

Keep working at your day job while you develop your great idea. Mozart often had to scramble to make a living. He gave many piano lessons. He attended concerts and gave piano recitals. He visited wealthy people to endeavour to gain patronage. Often, he would arrive home at 11 pm and then start composing for a couple of hours. He did not let the demands of the day job stop him from pursuing his genius.

Manage your finances and your health. Although he was a genius with notes, Mozart was poor at managing money. When he had it, he was extravagant but, for long periods, he, his wife and family had little to eat and he was reduced to sending out begging letters. Had he managed his finances and health better, he might have lived beyond his meagre 35 years and given us even more masterpieces.

PYTHAGORAS

(570 – 495 BC)

Ancient Greek philosopher and mathematician

Pythagoras was one of the greatest mathematicians and philosophers amongst the ancient Greeks. He is credited with discovering the theorem that states that the square on the hypotenuse of a right-angled triangle is equal to the sum of the squares on the other two sides. He was one of the earliest scientists to propose that the Earth was a giant sphere revolving around the Sun. He taught that the workings of the Universe could be understood with the use of numbers and mathematics. He divided all numbers into odd and even. In some ways, he was the first great philosopher. His ideas greatly influenced subsequent Greek thinkers, including Plato, and, therefore, imbued much of the philosophy of Western civilisation.

According to legend, Pythagoras discovered that musical notes were based on mathematics, when he passed blacksmiths at work one day and heard the harmonies of the sounds from their anvils. He showed that the notes made by a vibrating string on a musical instrument have a mathematical relationship to the length of the string. He is credited with developing the theory of the 'harmony of the spheres'. This implies that the planets and stars move according to mathematical equations, which correspond to musical notes.

Pythagoras was born on the Aegean island of Samos in about 570 BC. He travelled throughout Greece, to Egypt and, possibly, as far as India. His home island of Samos was ruled by a tyrant, Polycrates, so Pythagoras fled to southern Italy, where he established a group who followed his ideas about religion and philosophy. It was both a school and sect, containing men and women. It was governed by his teachings and was very secretive. He died around 495 BC. The school of philosophy he founded continued until the fourth century BC.

INSIGHTS FOR INNOVATORS

Travel to muster knowledge and ideas. At a time when most people stayed in their home village, Pythagoras travelled widely to meet other thinkers and to learn fresh ideas. It is said that the Egyptians taught him geometry, the Phoenicians arithmetic, the Chaldeans astronomy and the Magians philosophy. Which bands of enterprising thinkers can you mix with to give you the range of skills you need? Do you travel to the same places on holiday or do you venture to strange places to learn and experience the novel?

Gather a band of brothers. We cannot be sure exactly which of the great ideas in mathematics came from Pythagoras himself and which from his school of acolytes. But, just like Edison, he is credited with the achievements, some of which probably arose from a college of thinkers that he had assembled. Surround yourself with constructive dissenters who will challenge and add to your views.

DID YOU KNOW ?... The Pythagoras' theorem, a fundamental relation in geometry, states that, in a right angle triangle, the square of the hypotenuse is equal to the sum of the squares of the other two sides. It is a message that we might use to contact an alien civilisation elsewhere in the Universe, as it is easy to show and recognise.

WILLIAM SHAKESPEARE

(1564 – 1616)

The greatest writer of all time

William Shakespeare was a poet, playwright, producer and entrepreneur, considered by many to be the greatest dramatist of all time. He wrote 37 plays and 154 sonnets. He worked the English language like no one before him or since. He was highly innovative and is credited with adding some 3,000 words, which he invented, to the language as well as countless well-known expressions. Most notably, his works expressed the range of human emotion and conflict in a richer and fuller way than ever before. He wrote all sorts of plays and scenes, including histories, comedies, romances and tragedies. He could write a wonderfully funny scene, such as the play in *A Midsummer Night's Dream* where the characters get their speeches completely wrong. He was equally brilliant at writing terrifying, pitiful or heartrending scenes, such as those in *Macbeth* or *King Lear*.

Millions of people read or watch his plays in their own languages around the world and thousands visit his birthplace in Stratford upon Avon in England. Yet little is known about his education or early life. We know that he came to London as a young man and there performed as an actor before becoming a professional writer. In 1599, Shakespeare and his partners built their own theatre, the Globe, on the bank of the River Thames. He bought other properties and, as a successful entrepreneur, he was able to pursue his interests as a poet and playwright.

Retelling stories was an essential part of William Shakespeare's art. *The Tempest* is the only one of his 37 plays whose plot cannot be traced back to earlier works. This has led to charges that he borrowed ideas from others. But that was common practice of the time. In those days, stories were shared as part of a common inheritance. Shakespeare was a master at reinventing and refining plots with rich characters and brilliant prose. He took existing writing styles of the day and adapted them to his own purposes, creating a much freer flow of words.

INSIGHTS FOR INNOVATORS

Borrow with pride. If borrowing and developing storylines from others was good enough for Shakespeare, then it is good enough for the rest of us. We cannot hope to match his brilliance, but we can benefit from his technique of taking a good idea and developing it with our own individual notions and style.

Make it up. Shakespeare did not follow conventions and rules. He made them up. When he found there was no word to express what he wanted to convey, he coined a new word. He invented and developed new forms of expression.

Take control in order to ensure your work is well presented. Sometimes, it is better to focus all your energies on your one field of expertise but, sometimes, it is better to manage the business side as well. Shakespeare and his colleagues built their own theatre, the Globe, and took over the Blackfriars indoor theatre to ensure good venues for their productions. He is known as a brilliant writer, but he was also a successful businessman and investor. This helped him show off his work to best effect.

PART 4
INVENTOR

ERIC MIGICOVSKY

(BORN 1986)

Founder and CEO of Pebble

The Canadian entrepreneur Eric Migicovsky took a year out from his degree course at Waterloo University, Ontario to study at Delft University of Technology in The Netherlands. Like most students there, he cycled every day and noticed a problem. You cannot answer your cell phone or read a message while cycling – unless you take both hands off the handlebar. He said, 'It occurred to me, hey, what if I could just do it on my wrist?'

He built a prototype of a 'smart' watch, which was linked through wireless to his mobile phone. It could display summary information about emails, messages and alerts – and tell the time. Migicovsky returned to Waterloo where he and some friends worked on early versions of the watch in their garage. He then went to California to present his business idea at Y Combinator, an incubator that invests a small amount of money into many start-ups. The founder of Y Combinator, Paul Graham, was impressed with Migicovsky and compared him to Steve Jobs.

The Canadian named his company Pebble Technology. He had a great idea, but needed more capital, so he turned to crowdfunding. The company launched a campaign on the crowdfunding site Kickstarter on 11 April 2012, with a target of $100,000. They made the deal attractive by offering investors a discounted future Pebble watch at $99 – a saving of $150 on the retail price. There was a frenzy of interest. Within two hours of the launch, the $100,000 goal had been met. Within six days, Pebble had raised over $4 million, making it the most funded project in the history of Kickstarter. On 18 May 2012, funding closed with $10 million pledged by 68,000 people.

The company is based in Palo Alto and sells a range of watches. Competitors, including Apple, soon arrived in the smart watch market.

Migicovsky released a software developers' kit to enable people to build applications for the Pebble watch. It became a platform for games, exercise monitoring and information feeds, such as stock prices, traffic and weather. By 2014, the Pebble store had over 1,000 applications.

INSIGHTS FOR INNOVATORS

How will you raise the finance you need for your innovative start-up? With crowdfunding, of course. Thousands of small businesses gain the investments they need from crowdfunding sites. Many companies offer incentives, such as discounted products or services. This means that not only do you get thousands of investors, you also get thousands of customers and evangelists for your new product.

Create a platform. If your product becomes something that others can use to provide their services, then you spread your influence and reach in the market. Provide the means whereby others can easily collaborate with you.

Spot a problem in your everyday life. Migicovsky knew that people referred to their smart phones several times an hour and often over 100 times a day. But there are times when it is inconvenient to use both hands. Many were aware of this, but he took action to fix it. If you, and many others, share a difficulty, then there is an opportunity for an innovation. Most will do nothing. Be the one who solves the problem.

GEORGE DE MESTRAL

(1907 – 1990)

Inventor of Velcro

On a beautiful summer's day in the 1940s, George de Mestral, a scientist and engineer, took his dog for a walk in the Swiss Alps. When they returned he noticed many small plant burrs clinging to his trousers and his dog's fur. He inspected one in detail under his microscope and saw that the seed-bearing burr had many small hooks, which enabled it to attach to clothes or to the fur of animals. From this insight, he conceived a new way to fasten materials together.

He developed a synthetic fastening system that mimicked the tiny hooks and loops of the burrs. He called it Velcro from the French words *velours* and *crochet* (velvet and hooks). He worked in engineering, not textiles, but he could see great potential for his new idea there. He showed his invention to various people, but was met with ridicule and rejection. Initially, he made it from cotton but, after many trials, he found that nylon was a superior material. He patented his invention in 1955 and then tried to sell the concept of what he called a 'zipperless zipper'. There were no takers. But, eventually, in the 1960s, NASA adopted the fastening for use on space suits. Skiers and scuba divers started to use Velcro in their suits and, eventually, it became widely accepted by the fashion industry.

George de Mestral was born and raised near Lake Geneva in Switzerland. As a child, he displayed a talent for technical creativity. At the age of 12, he gained a patent for a type of model plane. He graduated as an electrical engineer. He sold the Velcro patent to the Velcro Company, which went on to make millions of the fastenings. Afterwards, de Mestral continued to be innovative and was granted patents for other inventions, including a hygrometer for measuring humidity and an asparagus peeler. He died in 1990.

INSIGHTS FOR
INNOVATORS

Be curious about unusual things. Most people would simply be annoyed that their clothing had many burrs that were difficult to remove. However, these irritating attachments spurred de Mestral's curiosity. He saw that nature had perfected a powerful way of affixing things and he copied it.

Be persistent. De Mestral had his eureka moment in the 1940s, but it was 20 years later that his innovation finally took hold. He had to ignore the people who scoffed at him. He had to continue to develop and refine the idea until it worked really well. Finally, he gave us something that is now in everyday use all over the world.

Mimic nature. Many great inventions are based on ideas from the natural world adapted for the man-made world. See Alexander Graham Bell for another example.

SIR HIRAM MAXIM

MAXIM

(1840 – 1916)

Inventor of the machine gun

When Hiram Maxim went pigeon shooting, he noticed two problems. One was the strong recoil of the rifle into his shoulder. The second was that he had to stop to reload the gun. He wondered if it was possible to use one problem to solve the other. He did so and invented the machine gun. The force from the recoil of a bullet was used to load the next bullet, close the breech and compress a spring. The gun was then ready for its next shot.

Sir Hiram Maxim was born in Maine in 1840. At 14, he became an apprentice coachbuilder. Subsequently, he worked in a machine shop and then as an instrument-maker and as a draughtsman.

He became a prolific inventor. He gained patents on mechanical devices, such as a pocket menthol inhaler, a mousetrap, hair-curling irons and steam pumps. He experimented with powered flight, but his large aircraft designs were failures. He did, however, create a highly successful amusement ride, the 'Captive Flying Machine'. When a furniture factory burned down, Maxim was asked how to stop similar fires. In response, he invented the first automatic fire sprinkler. It could soak the burning area with water and report the event to the fire station. He was responsible for installing the first electric lights in a New York City building and he even disputed Thomas Edison's claims to the invention of the lightbulb, based on his own discoveries.

He invented the machine gun in 1884. His company, the Maxim Gun Company, became part of Vickers Ltd, of which he became a director. The Vickers machine gun was the standard issue weapon in the British Army during the First World War.

In 1900, he became a British subject and was knighted by King Edward VII. He died in London in 1916. He was the holder of 122 US patents and 149 British patents.

Look for the solution inside the problem. Sometimes, there is an effective and economic solution waiting to be found inside the problem. Maxim used one problem of the rifle, the powerful recoil, to solve the other problem, how to load the next bullet. Before you look outside for solutions, see if any of the local resources can be utilised.

The more things you invent, the better your chance of a winner. Many of Maxim's inventions did not succeed – for example his aircraft. However, some did and the machine gun changed warfare completely. His dogged devotion to invention compares to that of his contemporary and rival, Thomas Edison. Persistence pays.

DID YOU KNOW?... You can see the only original version of Hiram Maxim's flying machine amusement ride, which is still in use, at the Pleasure Beach in Blackpool in the north of England. It was built in 1904.

JOHANNES GUTENBERG

(C. 1398 – 1468)

German craftsman who developed the printing press

Which invention or innovation has had the most positive impact on the development of civilisation and the greatest benefit for mankind? A strong contender is the printing press.

Johannes Gutenberg was a German blacksmith, goldsmith and printer who introduced the printing press and movable type into Europe. Before Gutenberg, all books had been hand written or stamped out with fixed wood blocks. This made books rare, expensive and prone to transcription errors. Knowledge was restricted to a handful of wealthy or religious people.

Gutenberg combined two existing ideas – the power of a wine press and the detail of a coin punch – to create the printing press. He developed movable type, which meant that the same page could be printed many times at low cost. The type could then be rearranged to print another page. The idea of pressing a raised image against paper had been around for some time – mainly in China. But Gutenberg was the first to enable a machine to mass-produce books. His inventions of the printing press and mechanical movable type started a revolution in communication throughout Europe. It facilitated the spread of knowledge in the form of printed books and pamphlets. This fuelled the Renaissance and the Reformation. There followed the Age of Enlightenment and the sharing of scientific knowledge. Furthermore, Gutenberg's printing press was the first step in the transition from an artisan-based society to one of manufacturing and mass production.

There were many details that Gutenberg had to master. He invented a process for mass-producing movable type based on new metal alloys. He developed a new oil-based ink. He adapted screw presses used for squeezing grapes. His great achievement was to combine all these components into a practical system for the mass production of printed books.

In Renaissance Europe, the arrival of inexpensive printed books started an era of mass communication, which permanently altered the structure of society. Revolutionary ideas flowed across the continent and challenged the powers of established political and religious elites. Many consider Gutenberg's printing press to be one of the most influential inventions in history. In 1997, *LIFE* magazine picked Gutenberg's invention as the most important of the second millennium. In terms of the impact on mass communication, the inventions of paper and the internet are the only two that come close to the printing press.

INSIGHTS FOR INNOVATORS

Combine. Many great innovations are really recombinations of existing ideas. Gutenberg's great innovation involved combining the humble wine press and coin punch to make the mighty printing press.

The idea alone is not sufficient; you have to be able to build it. Forms of movable type had been used in Asia hundreds of years earlier, but Gutenberg's innovation was developing a casting system and metal alloys, which made mass production practical. He went on to print beautiful Bibles and other religious books. You have to master the details in order to demonstrate that your innovation works.

Innovations often have unintended and dramatic consequences. Gutenberg presses were used originally to print the Bible in Latin. However, printing presses were, subsequently, used to print seditious, heretical and revolutionary texts, which disrupted society and ushered in a new age. Be aware that the more fundamental your innovation the more unexpected consequences may result.

JOHN HARRISON

(1693 – 1776)

Master clockmaker and winner of the world's first great crowdsourced competition

O n 22 October 1707, a fleet of the Royal Navy, under the command of Admiral Sir Cloudesley Shovell, encountered severe weather near the Scilly Isles off the southwest coast of England. Four ships ran aground and were wrecked, with the loss of 1,400 sailors, including Shovell himself. The main cause of the disaster was the inability of the seamen to calculate their positions accurately. In those days, navigators had great difficulty in ascertaining their longitude – how far east or west they were.

The Scilly naval disaster was one of the worst catastrophes at sea and caused much consternation in Britain. So much so, that, in 1714, the British Parliament passed the Longitude Act, offering a series of rewards of up to £20,000 for anyone who could find a simple, precise and practical way of determining a ship's longitude. It was the first example of a major public crowdsourced competition and the prize was huge by the standards of the day (equivalent to almost £3 million today).

John Harrison was a self-educated carpenter and clockmaker from Yorkshire, who dedicated his life to solving the longitude problem. He was born near Wakefield in 1693, the son of a carpenter. As a boy, he was always fascinated by clocks and he built his first longcase clock at the age of 20. As befits a carpenter, it was made almost entirely of wood. Over the next decades, he introduced several significant innovations in clock design so that, by the late 1720s, Harrison and his brother James were making the most accurate clocks in the world.

His innovations included the gridiron pendulum, made of brass and iron rods in order to eliminate thermal expansion, and the grasshopper escapement – a brilliant invention to control the release of the clock's power. Unlike other clocks of the day, his were designed to be practically frictionless and required no lubricants.

Longitude is the measure of the location of a place on Earth east or west of a north-south line, such as the prime meridian, which runs through Greenwich in London. It ranges up to 180°

eastward and −180° westward. There were two main approaches to the problem of establishing exact longitude at sea. One was based on astronomical observations and lunar distances, but these were difficult and did not give enough precision. The other approach was based on timekeeping. For each 15° west one sails, the day starts and ends one hour later, so, if you can measure noon from the position of the sun where you are and you know the time at the place you left, then you can calculate exactly how far east or west you have travelled. The problem was how to produce a clock that was not affected by the motion of the ship or the changes in temperature, pressure and humidity on the journey. These variables had defeated many fine clockmakers. Sir Isaac Newton was amongst many who thought that a sufficiently accurate clock could not be built.

In 1730, Harrison moved to London and started the design of a marine clock to compete for the Longitude Prize. He spent time networking and raising finance. He recruited some powerful allies, including Edmond Halley, the Astronomer Royal, and George Graham, the country's leading clockmaker.

It took Harrison five years to build his first Sea Clock (H1, as it is known). He showed it to members of the influential Royal Society (of Sciences) who helped him present it to the Board of Longitude, the body authorised to award the prize. They were impressed and asked for a sea trial. This took place in 1736 on a voyage from London to Lisbon and back. The clock lost time on the outward voyage, but proved very accurate on the return trip.

The Board of Longitude was impressed and granted Harrison £500 for further development. He started the design of a second sea clock. In 1741, after three years of development, it was ready for a sea trial but, by then, Britain was at war with Spain and the invention was considered too important to risk capture by the Spanish. In any event, Harrison was dissatisfied with the design of H2 and used the hiatus to start work on a new clock, H3. He spent a further 17 years trying to perfect this clock but, despite incorporating many ingenious new features, he was unable to get it to perform with complete accuracy in a maritime environment. Eventually, he reached the conclusion that a watch design would be superior in performance and practicability. His insight was that a watch with a smaller balance than a clock could oscillate at a higher frequency and give greater accuracy.

In 1759, with the help of some of London's finest craftsmen, Harrison built his masterpiece, the world's first truly accurate marine watch (H4). It was a complex and highly novel design. He demonstrated how it could be used to calculate longitude.

Harrison was 68 years old when the watch was sent on transatlantic trial in 1761. It lost just 5 seconds in 81 days on the outward journey to Jamaica. Everyone expected the prize to be awarded, but the Board considered that the result might have been down to luck and demanded another trial. Harrison, his family and supporters were outraged, but the second trial went ahead, this time to Barbados and, once again, the watch proved accurate, losing just 37 seconds. Again, his opponents on the Board attributed the results to luck and refused to pay out. The matter was raised in Parliament, which offered Harrison £10,000 in compensation.

Harrison requested an audience with King George III, who took his side. The King's own tests showed that Harrison's watch was accurate to within one third of a second per day. Eventually, when he was 80 years old, and following pressure from the King, Parliament granted him a further £8,750, but neither he nor anyone else ever received the full Longitude Prize. He died on his 83rd birthday, 24 March 1776.

Harrison's marine chronometer was widely adopted in the years that followed. Captain Cook depended on it when mapping his discovery of Australia and the Pacific islands.

INSIGHTS FOR INNOVATORS

Persist. Harrison showed enormous tenacity and determination in pursuit of his goal. Despite many setbacks and injustices, he kept focused on refining and improving his designs and their manufacture. He dedicated his life to solving the longitude problem and he succeeded.

There is an old saying, 'It is not what you know, it is who you know'. Use your contacts. Harrison made use of his networks, collaborators and important contacts to raise finance and gain influence. He lobbied the King of England to gain his support. He could not have achieved what he did by working as a lone inventor. Who can help you make your innovation a commercial success?

Be prepared for a complete redesign. Harrison switched from a large clock to a smaller watch. His redesign improved performance and usability. Even if you have put tremendous effort into your design, you may have to rethink and start over again.

JOHN SIPE

(1859 – 1936)

Inventor of the siping process

John Sipe worked in an abattoir in the USA in the 1920s. Like other workers there, he found that he kept slipping on the wet and bloody floors. His shoes were too slippery, so he took his knife and cut thin slits across the rubber soles. He found that the shoes now gave a much better grip. In 1923, he took out a patent on the process and called it siping, with the slits called sipes. He thought it could improve the grip of car tyres and he was right but, unfortunately for him, the solid rubber tyres of the day had poor wet grip, even with sipes. Sipe died in 1936. His son, Harry E. Sipe, promoted the use of sipes in the USA for the new low-pressure balloon tyres around 1939.

Siping was not widely adopted by the motor industry until the 1950s, when pneumatic tyres with superior tread compounds were developed. They were much better suited to the process of siping. On roads covered with snow, ice or water, sipes in tyres significantly improve traction. A 1978 study by the US National Safety Council found that, on ice, siping improved stopping distances by 22 per cent and rolling traction by 28 per cent.

The car tyre industry and Formula One, in particular, developed siping and, nowadays, leading shoe manufacturers borrow ideas from racing car tyres to make their shoe soles grip better – so the idea has come full circle. Incidentally, the reason the sipes work is not because they carry water away; they make the sole much more flexible and allow a bigger area of contact and grip.

INSIGHTS FOR INNOVATORS

Sometimes, a minor innovation in one field can become a major one in a different field. John Sipe's invention made a small impact with shoes, but a huge one with car tyres. So, look outside your first field of endeavour to see if your innovation might be of greater value elsewhere.

▶

It can take a long time for a truly radical idea to become widely adopted. Be patient but maintain your patent and guard your intellectual property.

DID YOU KNOW ?... The Chinese city of Siping in Jilin Province has a population of 3.5 million. It was the site of a major battle in 1946 during the Chinese Civil War. It has no connection whatsoever with John Sipe.

JORGE ODÓN

(BORN 1952)

Inventor of the Odón device

Jorge Odón is an Argentinian car mechanic who invented a simple appliance that could save millions of lives of mothers and babies. He was shown a YouTube video of a trick to remove a cork from inside a bottle. The secret is to insert a plastic bag into the bottle, inflate the bag around the cork and then pull it out. He was fascinated and he won a bet by demonstrating the trick to a friend. Later that night, he had a brainwave – he could use the same principle that extracted the cork from the bottle to extract a baby during a difficult childbirth. He developed the idea and discussed it with people – most of whom thought he was crazy. But he persisted. He built a prototype using a glass jar, his daughter's toy doll and a fabric bag sewn by his wife.

In 2006, he patented the concept and gained the support of a leading obstetrician in Buenos Aires, Dr Javier Schvartzman, who helped him develop and improve the device. This gained the attention of the World Health Organization, whose chief coordinator for maternal health, Dr Mario Merialdi, was intrigued by the idea.

When the doctor or midwife activates the device, two plastic sleeves go over the baby's head, separating it from the birth canal. A little air is pumped into the sleeves, which inflate and grasp the head. The smooth plastic container is then pulled out. The World Health Organization says the device should be safer and easier to apply than a forceps, vacuum extractor or C-section operation, with less risk of infection.

Over 5 million babies and over a quarter of a million mothers die in childbirth every year – mainly in the developing world. Odón's invention could, potentially, save many of these lives because it is inexpensive and relatively easy to use. The product will be manufactured by Becton Dickinson and will be available at low cost in developing countries.

Jorge Odón is now celebrated for his invention. He said, 'I woke up one night with this idea; it almost felt magical. What I cannot understand is how I came up with a solution to help babies be born. I'm moved by the potential of this invention and I'm especially grateful to the doctors who first believed in me.'

INSIGHTS FOR INNOVATORS

Take a different view. We tend to think of childbirth as something biological or medical. But Odón approached the problem from the point of view of a mechanical engineer. By examining the mechanical process, he was able to conceive a mechanical device for its improvement.

Spot a weird connection. Odón watched a video of a cork in a bottle and saw an analogy with a baby in the birth canal. A solution in one field can be applied in another, if the connection can be found.

Outsiders can find radical solutions. Odón knew nothing about obstetrics, but this turned out to be an advantage. He thought like a mechanical engineer, not a doctor.

A radical idea initially looks absurd and needs support. Putting a plastic bag around a baby in the birth canal sounded ridiculous at first, so the open-minded support of Schvartzman and Merialdi was crucial to the survival and development of the idea.

LOUISE BRAILLE

(1809 – 1852)

The boy who enabled the blind to read

L ouis Braille was born in 1809 in Coupvray, a village near Paris. His father was a saddler and little Louis liked to play in his father's workshop. Unfortunately, at the age of three, he accidentally pushed a sharp tool called an awl into his eye. His eye became infected. The infection spread to his other eye, leaving the small child completely blind. Despite this terrible setback, Louis went to the local school and proved an avid pupil. He was a quick learner and a diligent student, despite his disability. At the age of 10, he won a scholarship to the only school for the blind in France, the Royal Institute for Blind Youth in Paris.

The school was run by Valentin Haüy, who had developed a system to enable blind people to read. He printed books using regular letters, which were raised and embossed so that the reader could feel their shapes. It was a method designed by sighted people. Blind people found it slow and clumsy, but it worked. The books were large, heavy and expensive to produce, so the school had only a handful.

Blind people were effectively excluded from the world of learning and written communication because the only books they could experience were costly and cumbersome. Louis Braille was determined to find a better way for the blind to read. In 1821, at the age of 12, he learned of a communication system invented by a captain in the French Army, Charles Barbier. If a soldier lit a match at night to read a message, then the light became a target for an enemy sniper, so Barbier devised a code that could be read in the dark. It consisted of dots and dashes raised on thick paper. It was complex and difficult to use, but Braille immediately saw the potential of the idea.

Braille spent many hours experimenting with the concept and developed a much better system by 1824, when he was just 15. He rotated the Barbier design and simplified it. He dropped the dashes and used two standard columns containing a total of six dots. His most important improvement was to create a cell that could be recognised with a single touch of a finger. He published his system in 1829 and printed the first book using it.

After graduation, he stayed at the school as first an assistant and then a teacher. He was a very gifted musician, being an accomplished cellist and organist. He played the organ at many churches in Paris.

Despite his failing health, he continued to refine and develop his system and he incorporated mathematical symbols and musical notation. He was highly respected and admired by pupils and staff at the school, but his new writing system was not adopted by the school or elsewhere. Indeed, the governors of the school and traditional educators opposed it.

He died of consumption in 1852 aged 43. After his death, pupils at the Institute insisted that his system be used there and its advantages became apparent. It spread first through the French-speaking world and gradually beyond. A universal braille code for English was formalised in 1932 and it has now been adopted officially by schools for the blind throughout the world. There are now braille computer terminals and email systems. The braille system has proved an invaluable aid to blind people everywhere.

INSIGHTS FOR INNOVATORS

Thoroughly understand the needs of your customers. Many well-meaning people with sight had tried to help blind people to read using ideas such as raised letters. Louis Braille had a deeper understanding of what it meant to be blind and he used that to devise a superior solution.

Adapt an impractical idea and make it practical. Make an existing idea better. Braille took the Barbier idea, which was clever but ineffective, and transformed it into something pragmatic and realistic.

Be patient. It can take years for great innovations to be acknowledged. Braille's brilliance was ignored during his lifetime, but it is recognised worldwide today. He is an inspiration to us all.

MARTIN COOPER

(BORN 1928)

Inventor of the mobile phone

M artin Cooper led the team at Motorola that developed the world's first handheld mobile phone. He was born in 1928 and served as a submarine officer in the US Navy during the Korean War before taking a degree in Electrical Engineering from Illinois Institute of Technology (IIT). In 1954, he joined Motorola and worked on pagers and then car phones using cellular technology. At that stage, the car phones were mobile only in the sense that they moved when the car did.

In the early 1970s, Cooper was worried that Motorola's great rival AT&T was gaining a lead in car phone technology and was lobbying the Federal Communications Commission (FCC) for frequency space for its car phone network. AT&T was larger than Motorola and had much greater research resources, but the competitive Cooper wanted to challenge, and even leapfrog, the giant. He has said that watching Captain Kirk using his communicator on the television show *Star Trek* inspired him with a stunning idea – to develop a handheld mobile phone. He and his team took only 90 days, in 1973, to create the first portable cellular phone prototype.

Martin Cooper was not just a clever engineer. He also understood the power of public relations. He called a press conference. On 3 April 1973, on Sixth Avenue in New York City, in front of a group of amazed journalists, Cooper made the first public phone call from a prototype handheld cellular phone. Showing remarkable chutzpah, he made that first call to Joel Engel, head of research at AT&T Bell Labs, to inform his rivals that they were well behind. He then allowed some of the reporters to make phone calls to anyone of their choosing to prove how the cell phone worked. The resulting publicity was a sensation.

Cooper later said, 'As I walked down the street while talking on the phone, sophisticated New Yorkers gaped at the sight of someone actually moving around while making a phone call. Remember that, in 1973, there weren't cordless telephones, let alone cellular phones. I made numerous calls, including one where I crossed the street while talking to a New York radio reporter – probably one of the more dangerous things I have ever done in my life.'

The original Motorola DynaTAC handset weighed a hefty 1 kg (2.2 lb) and had very restricted talk time. Cooper later joked, 'The battery lifetime was 20 minutes, but that wasn't really a big problem because you couldn't hold the phone up for that long.' Because of the infrastructure needed, it took a full 10 years before the first commercial cell phone, the DynaTAC 8000x, was launched in 1983. This phone weighed 1.1 lb, had 30 minutes of battery life and was priced at $3,995 – around $10,000 in today's prices.

Cooper is the recipient of many awards and he also sits on committees of the US Federal Communications Commission and the United States Department of Commerce.

INSIGHTS FOR INNOVATORS

An insight for an innovation can come from anywhere. It was while watching *Star Trek* on TV that Cooper had his brainwave. He saw something from a science fiction show and thought, 'Why not?' How can you exploit someone else's imaginative notion and turn it into reality? Books, magazines, films, TV shows, radio and the internet are awash with ideas that could prompt your innovation, if you can put together a clever concept and a customer need.

Use a brazen stunt to launch your big idea. Cooper did not just issue a press release. He organised a press conference on a busy New York street and made the world's first mobile phone call to his rival at AT&T. He let journalists try his new invention. The trick gained worldwide media coverage.

DID YOU KNOW?... The *Star Trek* series foreshadowed many other innovative ideas and inspired other inventors. Ed Roberts, who invented the first home computer, the Altair 8800, named it after the Altair Solar System in a *Star Trek* episode.

NICK D'ALOISIO

(BORN 1995)

Young internet entrepreneur

Nick D'Aloisio is the son of a lawyer and an investment banker, who had a brainwave while studying for his school exams. He was a 16-year-old London schoolboy when, in 2011, he invented a mobile phone app called Summly. He said, 'I was revising for a history exam and using Google, clicking in and out of search results, and it seemed quite inefficient. If I found myself on a site that was interesting, I was reading it and that was wasting time. I thought that what I needed was a way of simplifying and summarising these web searches. Google has Instant Preview, but that is just an image of the page. What I wanted was a content preview.' He created an application that summarises text documents into bullet points that can be read easily on the small screen of a mobile phone.

Within a few weeks, his iPhone app was downloaded over 100,000 times. He attracted attention from investors in Silicon Valley and China. In March 2013, he sold his application to Yahoo for a reported $30 million, making him one of the youngest self-made millionaires ever. He won the *Wall Street Journal* 'Innovator of the Year' title. Until he went to Oxford University in October 2015 to study Computer Science and Philosophy, D'Aloisio led the Yahoo News Digest, which won the 2014 Apple Design Award. In his summer vacation of 2015, he was the 'Entrepreneur in Residence' at Airbnb.

INSIGHTS FOR
INNOVATORS

You are never too young (or too old) to start your own business. If you have a great idea and see an opportunity for it, then go for it. Many young entrepreneurs are starting businesses, especially in the fields of mobile phone and internet applications and games.

▶

Necessity is the mother of invention, but pain can be the father of innovation. Whenever you or your customer has a problem, an inconvenience, a difficulty or a pain, there is an opportunity for innovation. A new product or service is called for to alleviate the pain. D'Aloisio created the app because of the problems he had scanning documents he was reviewing for his studies.

Try asking a teenager. Get some input from a digital native. Ask a tech-savvy teenager how they would tackle the issue that is stumping you. Many older executives now have a young techie as a reverse mentor to advise them on issues such as social media and new technology.

PERCY SPENCER

(1894 – 1970)

Inventor of the microwave oven

Percy Spencer was a self-taught physicist with a keen interest in electricity and its uses. One day, in 1946, while working with an active radar tube, he felt a tingling in his pocket and noticed the chocolate bar he kept there had melted. This phenomenon had been observed before, but Spencer was the first person to investigate it. He experimented by placing foods near a source of electromagnetic microwave radiation. He found that popcorn was quickly cooked and that an egg exploded.

He went on to develop the world's first microwave oven, using a metal box and a high density magnetron that emitted microwaves. His employers, the defence contractors Raytheon, filed a patent in 1945 for a microwave cooking oven and, in 1947, they produced the first commercial product, the Radarange. It cost about $2,500 and weighed 750 lbs. Affordable microwave ovens came onto the market 20 years later.

Spencer received no royalties for his invention, but Raytheon paid him a gratuity of $2, the company's standard token payment to all employees who filed patents.

Percy Lebaron Spencer was born in Maine in 1894. His father died when the boy was one and he was brought up by his aunt and uncle. He left school at 12 to work in a mill. At 18, he joined the US Navy, where he learnt wireless communications. He had no formal education, but taught himself mathematics, science and technology. In 1939, he joined the defence contractor Raytheon to build radar equipment. He rose to become senior vice president and a senior member of the Board of Directors at Raytheon. In the course of his work, he filed 300 patents. He was awarded the Distinguished Public Service Award, Fellowship in the American Academy of Arts and Sciences, and an honorary Doctor of Science from the University of Massachusetts.

INSIGHTS FOR INNOVATORS

Harness serendipity. Great innovators use the stimulus of random events to spur their imagination. Then they take action to turn ideas into experiments. Spencer observed the melting of the chocolate bar and then explored the actions of microwave radiation on foods. Do not treat every unexpected event as an annoyance. Sometimes, serendipity hands you an opportunity, if you are open minded.

Teach yourself the skills you need. We all need to keep reskilling and learning new methods and technologies. Spencer did this all his life. He kept learning and kept inventing. We all should do the same.

The commercialisation of an invention can take many years. As is the case with many inventors, Spencer had to wait a long time before he saw his great idea produced for the mass market. Patience is needed. It may be small consolation, but recognition for great ideas eventually materialises.

TED HOFF

(BORN 1937)

Inventor of the microprocessor

Marcian Edward Hoff (known as Ted) received a bachelor's degree in Electrical Engineering from the Rensselaer Polytechnic Institute in 1958 and PhD from Stanford in 1962. He joined Intel in 1968 as employee number 12.

At that time, Intel made electronic memory components. A Japanese client, Busicom, asked Intel to make 12 different semiconductor circuits to handle the 12 functions in its calculator. The job was given to Hoff, who studied the designs and thought there might be a better way to solve the problem. He approached his boss, Robert Noyce, chairman of Intel, with a proposal. Instead of 12 separate circuits, they could construct one circuit that could be programmed to perform all 12 functions. This would be smaller and much more adaptable. Noyce, to his credit, was enthusiastic about the idea. However, the client, Busicom, was not. They wanted to stick to the current approach. Eventually, Hoff and his colleagues persuaded Busicom to accept the idea.

Hoff, together with Frederico Faggin and Stanley Mazor, created the world's first microprocessor, the Intel 4004. They realised that they had created something very special but, unfortunately, the contract they had with Busicom meant that the Japanese company owned the design. Noyce flew to Japan and bought back the rights for $60,000.

The first microprocessors were industrial controllers, but they grew faster, denser and smarter. Nowadays, every device from a phone to a washing machine contains microprocessors. The original decision to try Hoff's idea has fuelled the growth of Intel into a multi-billion-dollar giant.

Hoff was inducted into the National Inventors Hall of Fame in 1996 and received the National Medal of Technology and Innovation in 2009 from President Barack Obama. He was made a Fellow of the Computer History Museum in 2009 'for his work as part of the team that developed the Intel 4004, the world's first commercial microprocessor'.

INSIGHTS FOR INNOVATORS

Do not always do what the customer asks. Most bosses would have rejected Hoff's idea as a distraction. They would have given the customer what they asked for. However, Hoff and Noyce were curious to try an innovative approach and it paid off.

Look for a better way to solve the problem. There is always a different way to solve a problem and, sometimes, the different way proves a better way – but you find out only if you try it.

If you are fortunate enough to have someone brilliant working for you, then give them the freedom to accomplish the brilliant. Noyce had the confidence to let Hoff run with his radical idea. Most managers would not. Give your best people space, resources and freedom from overbearing supervision so that they can succeed.

Thomas Edison was one of the world's greatest inventors. He was born in Milan, Ohio in 1847. As a child, he showed great curiosity and imagination – his teachers complained that he was continually asking questions. At the age of 10, he ran his own vegetable stall so that he could make money to buy chemicals for his chemistry experiments.

When he was 12, he sold fruit and magazines to commuters on a train and then set up a printing press in the train to print up-to-date information for travellers. Unfortunately, one of his bottles of chemicals broke and set fire to the carriage. The boy was fired. He learnt Morse code and telegraphy. He worked in various telegraph offices before going to New York, penniless and friendless. But he had a stroke of luck. He went into a telegraph company just as the telegraph stopped working. He was the only one there who could fix it and the boss was so pleased that he gave Edison a job. He then designed a stock ticker for relaying information about share prices. He sold the design for a large sum and decided to go into invention full time.

In 1877, he invented the gramophone (or phonograph as it was called), using a wax drum to record and play back sounds. He developed an improved typewriter. He and his team of scientists and technicians then went on to invent the electric light, the nickel-iron battery, a telephone mouthpiece, a dictating machine, a vote recorder and a prototype video camera. His many discoveries and inventions led to great advances in the use of electricity and in early electronics.

He introduced the concepts of large-scale teamwork and mass production to the business of invention and, consequently, he is credited with the creation of the first industrial research laboratory.

Edison is recognised as the world's most prolific inventor. He held some 1,090 patents in his name. His inventions had enormous significance, leading to the widespread use of electric light and power, telecommunications, sound recording and motion pictures.

There is no substitute for hard work. Edison famously said, 'Genius is 1 per cent inspiration and 99 per cent perspiration.' He was an incredibly hard worker and often would go without food or sleep, if he was working on a tricky problem.

Gather a team with the mix of skills needed to implement innovation. Although Edison is remembered as the supreme inventor, much of his success was based on his ability to recruit, motivate and manage a great team of engineers, technicians and scientists. The team magnified his genius and turned great ideas into working systems.

Carry out many, many experiments. Edison was renowned for the high number of scientific trials he undertook. His most famous quote is, 'I have not failed. I've just found 10,000 ways that won't work.' He treated each unsuccessful experiment as a learning experience. Sometimes, you need to dig a lot of ground to find a diamond.

TREVOR BAYLIS

(BORN 1937)

Inventor of the clockwork radio

Trevor Baylis was born in London. As a boy, he was a keen swimmer and narrowly missed selection for the UK 1956 Olympic swimming team. He studied engineering at a technical college. After serving as a physical training instructor in the army, he worked for a firm selling swimming pools.

He gave swimming and diving displays and became a stunt man and professional swimmer. He performed high dives into small glass-sided tanks and accomplished underwater escapes to entertain crowds. It was dangerous work and he knew several performers who had suffered injuries or become disabled. He had always been an inventor and, in 1985, he set up a company, Orange Aids, to develop products for the disabled.

In 1991, he watched a television programme about the spread of AIDS in Africa. He learnt that there was a desperate need to educate and inform people about the disease and how to prevent its transmission. Radio broadcasts would be an ideal way to do this, but many poor did not have electricity in their homes or could not afford to buy batteries for a radio. Before the programme had finished, he went to his workshop and built a prototype wind-up radio. He used the clockwork mechanism from a music box to drive an electric motor from a toy car to power a small transistor radio. He developed the idea so that, instead of using batteries or mains electricity, the listener would wind a clockwork crank. This stored energy in a spring that drove the generator that operated the radio. In 1992, he took out a patent on the idea and then approached many different people and companies to try to get the product into production and distribution. Everywhere he went, he was met with incredulity and rejection.

However, in 1994, his novel idea was shown on an episode of the BBC TV programme *Tomorrow's World*. He found investors and, with their backing, he started a company, Freeplay Energy, to make clockwork radios. The product proved popular in the developing world. Baylis was celebrated as a great inventor. In 1996, he received the World Vision Award for Development Initiative and the Freeplay radio was awarded the BBC Design Award for Best Product and Best Design. He met Queen Elizabeth II and Nelson Mandela and travelled to Africa to produce a documentary about his life.

He continued to invent. He developed some 'electric shoes', so that a walker charges a small battery that could power a cell phone or other small device. In 2001, he demonstrated them by making a 100-mile walk across the Namib Desert in Africa.

He founded a company, Trevor Baylis Brands, to help inventors develop and protect their inventions. It was inspired by the difficulties he had experienced.

Baylis received awards and honours, including honorary degrees and the OBE and CBE from the Queen. However, whilst he was a great inventor, he was not a successful businessman and never made a substantial personal return from his many ventures. He sold his shares in Freeplay cheaply and lost his patent for the clockwork radio. He said, 'I was very foolish. I didn't protect my product properly and allowed other people to take my product away.'

INSIGHTS FOR INNOVATORS

Take a step backwards to find a simpler way. To many people, the idea of a clockwork radio seemed retrograde and silly. It was easy to find fault with the idea. The radio would stop in the middle of a programme and need winding. The wind-up mechanism made the radio bulky. Surely batteries were simpler. From a Western viewpoint, these were all valid points but, in the poorest parts of

Africa, they were not. Sometimes, a cheaper and less sophisticated solution will find a big market.

Use mass media to gain exposure. Baylis could not sell his idea to the companies and backers he approached. It took a TV appearance for the clockwork radio to gain support. If the normal routes do not work, then try something radical – and big.

Protect your invention. Secure your patents and renew them. Retain some equity in the companies you create. Be businesslike and secure proper agreements. Baylis admitted, 'I had been used to doing business on a handshake and my word of honour, and I made the error of actually believing what the men in the pin-striped suits told me.'

PART 5
MAVERICK

Anita Roddick opened the first Body Shop store in Brighton, England in 1976 to provide an income for herself and her two daughters while her husband was away trekking in South America. The Body Shop was remarkably different from conventional cosmetic stores at the time. It offered quality skin care products in plain refillable containers and sample sizes with no advertising or hype. Roddick created a range of products based on natural ingredients at a time when people were increasingly anxious over the use of chemicals. She appealed to her customers' concern for the environment. She offered discounted refills to customers who brought back their empty containers. This fresh approach proved a storming success. Her husband joined the business on his return. They opened more shops – by 1991, they had 700 and Anita was given the World Vision Award for Development Initiative.

Anita and Gordon Roddick took The Body Shop public in 1984. After just one day of trading, the stock doubled in value. It continued to climb over the next decade as hundreds of Body Shop franchises were launched across Europe and the USA. By 2004, there were 1,980 stores with over 77 million customers worldwide. In that year, The Body Shop was voted the second most trusted brand in the United Kingdom and ranked in the world's top 30 brands. In 2006, L'Oréal purchased The Body Shop for £652 million.

One of the causes of Roddick's success was her social activism. Her company was one of the first to prohibit the use of animal testing on products and was a leader in promoting fair trade with Third World countries. She became a high profile figure with her vociferous support for causes such as Greenpeace, Amnesty International and saving the rainforests. This approach generated free publicity and a loyal customer base. The company supported local community and environmental groups. The chain became a movement people believed in rather than just another commercial enterprise. In

1997, Anita Roddick launched a global campaign to raise self-esteem in women and to oppose the media stereotyping of women.

Although the company's approach looked like a dazzling business strategy, it was something that Roddick stumbled upon. She told *Third Way* magazine, 'The original Body Shop was a series of brilliant accidents. It had a great smell, it had a funky name. It was positioned between two funeral parlours; that always caused controversy. It was incredibly sensuous. We knew about storytelling then, so all the products had stories. We recycled everything, not because we were environmentally friendly, but because we didn't have enough bottles. It was a good idea. What was unique about it, with no intent at all, no marketing nous, was that it translated across cultures, across geographical barriers and social structures. It wasn't a sophisticated plan, it just happened like that.'

Roddick grew a single shop into an international empire. She showed that a company can gain loyal customers and succeed with simple products and environmentally friendly approaches and by eschewing expensive packaging and advertising.

INSIGHTS FOR INNOVATORS

Do the opposite. Swim against the tide. Anita Roddick deliberately did the reverse of what the industry leaders and experts did. She saw that cosmetic stores were stuffy places that sold toiletries, perfumes and medicinal creams in expensive packaging and pretty bottles. She did the opposite by packaging the goods in The Body Shop stores in cheap, plastic bottles with plain labels. The store gave refills. It saved costs and it made a statement that the contents of the packages were what mattered.

▶

Stand for what you believe in. Become a movement. The Body Shop differentiated itself by stating that it would never use animal testing in its product development. It was seen as natural, spiritual and in tune with an environmentally friendly consumer.

Generate publicity through activism and controversy. Roddick had a natural talent for reaping free publicity. The funeral parlour owners next door to her first shop complained that her store's name would hurt their business. So she went to the local press with a story saying the undertakers were intimidating a woman entrepreneur starting a business. As a result, many people came to the store to see what the fuss was about. Throughout her career, Roddick continued to be vocal on many high-profile causes.

DON ESTRIDGE

(1937 – 1985)

The 'father' of the IBM PC

Don Estridge was born in 1937 in Jacksonville, Florida. He gained a bachelor's degree in electrical engineering at the University of Florida. He worked for the army and then joined IBM, working in the 1960s at NASA's Goddard Space Flight Center.

The 1970s saw IBM dominate the mainframe computer arena, but smaller companies were nipping at its heels with mini-computers and home computers. IBM promoted Estridge to lead the team that developed its first mini-computer, the Series /1. It was not a great success and he was assigned a staff position. However, in 1980, he took charge of the IBM Entry Level Systems and was given the objective of developing an inexpensive personal computer to take on the upstarts like Atari, Apple and Commodore.

Estridge realised that he could not create a viable competitive product and bring it to market quickly, if he used standard IBM development processes. At that time, IBM maintained total control of all its manufacturing with proprietary designs from power supplies to integrated circuits to operating systems. If he followed the normal IBM procedures, the product would be far too expensive for the fast-growing consumer market.

Estridge decided to bypass the heavy-duty approach and, instead, to go outside the company for third-party components and software. Even more radically, Estridge opted for an 'open architecture'. He published the specifications of the IBM PC, thus enabling a burgeoning industry of suppliers of add-ons, hardware and software products. The product included expansion card slots specifically to take external offerings.

'When we started,' Estridge said, 'we were a dozen people who knew a little about personal computers.' The engineers in his small team had all come from the world of large computers and the biggest task was to get them to think completely differently about computers. 'The most important thing we learned was that how people reacted to a personal computer emotionally was almost more important than what they did with it,' he recalled. 'That was an entirely new lesson in computer design.'

In four months, Estridge and his team developed a prototype and, within one year, the IBM PC was on retail shelves, a record time for product development in the giant company. The product was launched in August 1981. Competitors initially were unworried because they were shipping higher specification machines of their own design, but the open architecture proved a key competitive advantage and the IBM product quickly came to dominate the market. Its success led to the formation of companies like Compaq and Dell, who specialised in 'PC clone' products.

Estridge was promoted several times at IBM and, in 1984, became vice president, manufacturing. He turned down a lucrative offer from Steve Jobs to become president of Apple Computers.

On 2 August 1985, Estridge and wife Mary Ann were killed when the plane they were travelling in crashed at Dallas. He was 48 years old. At the time of his death, the IBM PC group had grown to 10,000 employees and was grossing about $4.5 billion a year. If it had been a separate entity, it would have been the third largest computer company in the world behind IBM and DEC.

INSIGHTS FOR INNOVATORS

Tear up the rule book. Don Estridge broke all the standard operating procedures at IBM in order to ship a revolutionary product in record time. He decided that the only way to succeed was to break all the rules and move fast. What Estridge did was heresy within IBM, but it delivered dramatic results and he was applauded for it. Do not assume that big companies cannot be flexible – sometimes you have to be the rebel they need.

▶

Accept that failure is part of the process. Not all Estridge's ventures were successful. The Series /1 misfired. After the success of the PC, his team developed the PCjr home computer, which flopped. However, he was sanguine about it. 'You have to take risks in this business,' he said, 'or it's no fun.'

Design a platform not a product. The IBM PC was successful because its open architecture enabled companies and individuals to customise and adapt it to many varied uses. It became a platform for software and hardware developers. Try to develop something that others can build on and enhance. With luck, they will become supporters and evangelists.

HANNIBAL

(247 – 182 BC)

Rome's greatest enemy and one of the
finest military strategists of all time

Hannibal was an illustrious general of the North African state of Carthage, Rome's enemy and rival for control of the Mediterranean. His father was a Carthaginian general, Hamilcar, who made his nine-year-old son swear undying enmity for Rome. As a boy, Hannibal went to Spain, which was under Carthaginian control, and trained to be a soldier. At the age of 26, he was put in command of an army and led an attack on the city of Saguntum – near Valencia.

In 218 BC, he set out on an audacious invasion of Italy. He took a huge army of infantrymen and cavalry from Spain, across southern France and through the Alps to attack the Roman Empire from the north. His army included 38 battle-trained elephants, a weapon the Roman soldiers had never seen before. He had to fight off fierce ambushes by the local tribes and face ice, snow and avalanches. He lost thousands of men but, when he reached Italy, he caught the Romans completely unawares.

The Romans hurriedly sent an army to repel the invasion, but Hannibal defeated them at the Battle of Trebia (218 BC), thus gaining control of Northern Italy. He turned many of Rome's previous allies into his own. The next year, Hannibal crossed into Central Italy and defeated another Roman army at the battle of Trasimeno. A year later, Hannibal won his third great battle in Italy at Cannae. He opposed an army of 50,000 Romans. He drew up his army with his best soldiers on the flanks. He attacked with his centre to engage the Romans and then his centre retreated. The Romans followed into the centre of Hannibal's crescent, whereupon he commanded his flanks to close in on the Roman army, most of whom were killed or captured.

Hannibal's reputation as a brilliant and daring general inspired his troops and frightened his opponents. It has also enthused historians. His tactics of envelopment at the Battle of Cannae are renowned and studied in military academies to this day.

Hannibal continued to fight in Italy, but he never attacked the heavily fortified city of Rome. He could not get the supplies he needed from Carthage, but had to forage for local provisions. He was outnumbered and harried by the Romans, but displayed great leadership and clever military tactics to sustain his occupation of Italy for 15 years. In 203 BC, he was recalled to Carthage to fight against a Roman invasion led by Scipio. He was defeated by Scipio at the Battle of Zama in 202 BC. He continued to serve Carthage but, eventually, had to flee to Bithynia in Asia Minor. When the king of Bithynia was defeated in battle by the Romans, Hannibal chose to commit suicide rather than be captured by his arch enemies.

INSIGHTS FOR INNOVATORS

Use a new and unexpected weapon. Hannibal placed great value in his specially trained elephants, which struck terror into foes who had never seen this animal before. They roared as they trampled enemy troops and they had sharpened tusks to gouge horses and men.

Outflank your competition. Come at them from an unexpected direction. Hannibal crossing the Alps was one of the most daring ventures in military history. It was immensely difficult to take a huge army over freezing, tiny and precipitous mountain paths. However, the news that he had reached Northern Italy shocked and terrorised the Romans. We see many examples in business of companies bypassing competitors by using an alternate way to reach customers – think of Amazon versus bookstores.

DID YOU KNOW ?... Many generals have modelled their tactics on those of Hannibal – especially the encirclement he used at Cannae. However, the Second World War US General George Patton went further. He believed that he had been Hannibal in a previous life.

VISCOUNT HORATIO NELSON

(1758 – 1805)

Britain's greatest naval commander

On 21 October 1805, the French and Spanish fleets, consisting of 33 ships under the command of Admiral Villeneuve, were intercepted by a British fleet of 27 vessels under Admiral Nelson, off the coast of Cadiz in Spain. What followed, the Battle of Trafalgar, was to determine the balance of power on the high seas and across Europe. In those times, naval battles were fought by two opposing fleets, which lined up in parallel and fired canons at each other. The vessels were called 'ships of the line' for this reason. However, in this battle, Nelson employed a new tactic. He turned his ships through 90 degrees, organised them in 2 lines and sailed straight into the French and Spanish lines. The British ships presented a smaller target to enemy fire as they approached, but they could not fire back. However, once they broke through the line, they could fire deadly broadsides at close range.

This innovative approach worked brilliantly and gave Nelson his greatest triumph. Seventeen Franco-Spanish ships were captured and one was blown up. The British lost no ships, but their victory was marred by the death of Lord Nelson, who was shot by a French marksman.

Nelson was born in Norfolk, England, the sixth of eleven children. His father was a church rector. The boy joined the Navy at the age of 12 and, at 19, he was appointed a lieutenant. For most of his adult life, Britain was at war, often with France, so Nelson saw much active service. His courage in action and high skills of seamanship saw him promoted rapidly. He was given command of HMS *Albemarle* in 1781. He fought many actions and was wounded several times in combat. He lost the sight of his right eye during an engagement in Corsica. After his unsuccessful attempt to capture Santa Cruz de Tenerife, he suffered the loss of his right arm in an agonising amputation. He distinguished himself as a brilliant naval leader with his triumphs at the Battle of Cape St Vincent (1797), the Battle of the Nile (1798) and the Battle of Copenhagen (1801).

Nelson's death at Trafalgar secured his position as one of Britain's greatest heroes. He was revered for his inspirational leadership, superb grasp of strategy and innovative tactics. His memorial, Nelson's Column, towers over Trafalgar Square in the centre of London.

INSIGHTS FOR INNOVATORS

Change the point of attack. The idea of attacking the enemy line at right angles was suggested by a Scottish naval strategist, John Clerk. It was given the name 'crossing the T'. Nelson had the mettle to put it into practice in a strategically vital battle. It is no good having great ideas if you do not implement them.

Overcome adversity. Nelson suffered from chronic seasickness. He was afflicted with malaria, which laid him low for extended periods. He had one eye and one arm. By any measures, he was severely disabled. Yet, he did not make excuses or shirk responsibility. He rose to the most senior rank in the Royal Navy and, when called upon, he led his fleet brilliantly.

Inspire your team. Because he had risen up the ranks, Nelson understood the tribulations and needs of the ordinary seamen who served under him. He was known as a firm, fair and sympathetic leader who looked after the needs of his crew. He was decisive and skilled in naval tactics. He inspired confidence in subordinates and in his political masters alike.

JONATHAN SWIFT

(1667 – 1745)

Irish writer and satirist

Jonathan Swift was born in Dublin, Ireland in 1667. His father (who was also called Jonathan Swift) was a lawyer, who died just two months before the birth of his son. The baby's mother could not provide for him, so she handed him into the care of his uncle Godwin Swift, who was also an eminent lawyer. The boy went to grammar school and then, at the age of 14, to the University of Trinity College Dublin.

This was a time of great strife and upheaval. In 1688, the Catholic King of England, James II, was overthrown by the protestant William of Orange. Swift moved to England and became the secretary of a leading politician, Sir William Temple. He was ordained as an Anglican priest and later became dean of St Patrick's Cathedral in Dublin.

In 1704, Swift used a pseudonym to publish a short book, *A Tale of a Tub*. It was a witty parody of the divisions of Christian churches. It proved popular with the public, but not with the Church of England. He went on to write many essays, books and political pamphlets.

His masterpiece, *Gulliver's Travels*, was published in 1726. It was a popular story that contained many allegories for the political events of the times.

In 1729, he published a short book entitled *A Modest Proposal*, in which he suggested that poor people should sell their children to be eaten by rich people. He wrote, 'A young healthy child is a most delicious, nourishing and wholesome food, whether stewed, roasted, baked or boiled.' He went on to list the economic and social advantages of his suggestion. Many people, on hearing the idea, were deeply offended, though some took it seriously. Only later in the book did it become apparent that he was being intentionally provocative. He then laid out his proposed reforms to improve the plight of the poor and starving in society.

In his book *The Art of Creative Thinking*, Rod Judkins argues that Swift's outrageous provocation was justified. He said that Swift's book had had a profound impact, and that a sober and conventional proposal of reforms could have gone unnoticed. He also pointed out that Swift wanted something to happen and wanted to change things quickly, so he had taken a chance.

In his day, Swift was popular and notorious. He was a thorn in the side of the British political establishment. He is now revered as an Irish hero and as the foremost satirist in the history of English literature.

In 1745, Jonathan Swift died. He is buried in St Patrick's Cathedral in Dublin. He left most of his estate to found a hospital in Dublin for the mentally ill, which exists to this day.

INSIGHTS FOR INNOVATORS

If other methods fail to get your creative message noticed, then maybe you should try being annoying, irritating or even offensive. Swift's *Modest Proposal* was deliberately distasteful. It was a big risk. But innovators have to be risk takers. Dare you walk the precipice?

Wrap your radical message in a subtle way. Swift's book *Gulliver's Travels* was immensely popular from the day of its publication. It can be seen as a children's book or as an early piece of science fiction. However, within the book, there is a keen satire on the state of European governments and of petty differences between religions. Some see it as a work of philosophy on the corruption of mankind. Most books of the day were quite

▶

straightforward, but Swift intentionally innovated with an ambiguous book that works on different levels.

It is better to be notorious than to be anonymous. If you want to create waves, you have to do something that is noticed. Jonathan Swift, like Roy Lichtenstein, deliberately upset the establishment.

PHIL ROMANO

(BORN 1940)

Restaurateur and serial entrepreneur

P hil Romano is an Italian American who has started a series of restaurant chains. As a serial entrepreneur, he has launched some 25 different restaurant concepts that produce over $1.5 billion in annual revenues. Successful ventures include Cozymel's, Fuddruckers, EatZi's and Romano's Macaroni Grill. He has had his share of flops, too, including Baroni's, an expensive men's clothing retailer, and a seafood restaurant called Lobster Ranch.

In a recent interview in *Fortune* magazine, he tells how he financed the launch of Fuddruckers, a high-end burger restaurant. It was 1980, and he needed $150,000, but no bank would lend it to him. So, he sold 48 per cent of the business in the form of 10 shares for $15,000 each to wealthy customers. He retained 52 per cent. The chain was successful and, at its IPO in 1983, each of his investors recouped $3.4 million.

Romano now runs a restaurant start-up incubator called Trinity Groves.

When he started Romano's Macaroni Grill in San Antonio, Texas, he found that the restaurant was busy at weekends, but there was very little traffic in the early part of the week.

Romano decided that one Monday or Tuesday every month, all the food would be free, but he did not announce which day. People constantly called to ask, 'Is tonight the night?' They found out when they arrived. Word spread and the business increased dramatically.

Some doctor friends of Romano's developed a new design for a stent to open clogged arteries. Against the advice of his accountants, Romano provided $250,000 in angel funding to the group. A year later, the patent was sold to Johnson & Johnson. The invention went on to save many lives. It was also profitable for Romano.

He wanted to do something to help the poor and homeless. He started feeding them from a van and called the idea Hunger Busters. The soup kitchen on wheels grew to feed 3,000 street people every week.

INSIGHTS FOR INNOVATORS

Sometimes it pays to be unpredictable and play games with your customers. Phil Romano did not compete by doing more of what the others were doing. He did something unexpected. Standard management training dictates that you do not play games with your customers. You should deliver a predictable and expected outcome consistent with your brand. But Romano did something unpredictable and introduced a form of gamification. If the customers played along, sometimes they were rewarded with a free meal and then happily went on to tell all their friends. What can you do that is competitively unpredictable? Could you play a game with your customers?

Do something extra for those worse off. As a restaurant owner, Phil knew about providing hot food, so he found a way to do so for homeless people. Can you use your particular skills and innovations to help others? It is worthwhile in its own right, but also helps build your reputation and garners publicity.

STEVE JOBS

(1955 – 2011)

Business revolutionary and co-founder
of Apple Corporation

S teve Jobs was adopted at birth in 1955. He grew up in California. He dropped out of college, but voluntarily took a course in calligraphy. He found it beautiful and fascinating. The marriage of aesthetics and technology became his life-long obsession. He led a company that embodied the combination of art and science. He was an eclectic revolutionary. Computers, cell phones, tablets, films, animation, music and retail all felt the effects of his lateral thinking.

At the age of 21, Jobs founded Apple with Steve Wozniak in order to market the Apple I personal computer. It was followed by the Apple II, which was one of the first commercially successful mass-produced PCs. Jobs saw the potential of the graphical user interface and he introduced it in 1983 on the Apple Lisa, which flopped, and then, in 1984, on the Apple Macintosh, which was a breakthrough success. But he had a prickly personality and, in 1985, he was forced out of the company in a power struggle.

After leaving Apple, Jobs founded NeXT, a computer platform development company. He went on to fund the launch of a new company, Pixar, which became the leader in animation and visual effects for movies. It produced the first fully computer-animated film, *Toy Story*.

In 1997, Apple purchased NeXT, thereby enabling Jobs to, again, become Apple's CEO. At the time, the company was close to bankruptcy. Jobs worked with designer Jonathan Ive to develop a stunning sequence of new product blockbusters: the iMac, iTunes, Apple Stores, the iPod, the iTunes Store, the iPhone, the App Store, and the iPad.

In 2005, the iPod portable music player was Apple's best-selling product. It represented 45 per cent of their revenues. But CEO Steve Jobs was uncomfortable. He foresaw a looming threat. According to his biographer Walter Isaacson, Jobs said that the device that could eat our lunch was the cell phone. Because Apple lacked the technical skills in this field, he sought to collaborate with a dominant player in mobile telephony, Motorola.

However, this did not work well, so Jobs made the decision to go it alone. He empowered his team to design something radical and they did. They eschewed the keyboard as used by the then market leaders Blackberry and Nokia. Instead, they developed the touch screen. The Apple iPhone was launched in 2007 and became the market leader in the mobile phone market. By 2015, iPhone sales were 63 per cent of Apple's turnover whilst the iPod was down to less than 1 per cent.

Jobs was diagnosed with a pancreatic tumour in 2003 and, after a long struggle, he died in October 2011.

INSIGHTS FOR INNOVATORS

Technical excellence in your product is not sufficient. It is the combination of form and function that matters. Jobs understood that customers would love high-tech products, if they were beautiful as well as functional.

Jobs famously disdained focus groups. He believed that, if you asked customers what they wanted, they would request bland incremental improvements. He was convinced that the innovator should create something so different and wonderful that it would attract customers who never knew they wanted such a thing. The Apple iPad is a classic example.

Never be happy with your current successes. Each is temporary. Just like the iPod. Start planning your next great innovation.

Set impossibly high standards. Jobs was notoriously difficult to please – and, consequently, difficult to work for. He demanded something close to the impossible from his teams in terms of design functionality and deadlines. By reaching for the unreachable, he achieved the wonderful.

PART 6
PIONEER

AUGUSTE ESCOFFIER

(1846 – 1935)

Creator of the modern restaurant

Georges Auguste Escoffier was a French chef, restaurateur and culinary writer who transformed the restaurant eating experience and who remains a legendary figure amongst chefs and gourmets.

The Frenchman honed his culinary craft in Nice, Paris and Monte Carlo. In 1889, Richard D'Oyly Carte, the great impresario and owner of the new Savoy Hotel in London, invited Escoffier to London. He wanted him to take charge of the restaurant at the Savoy Hotel and establish its reputation as one of the best hotels in the world. Conventional preparation and serving of food at the time followed a time-honoured tradition. Many main and side dishes were placed on the table at the same time, giving the appearance of a sumptuous banquet. But the food quickly became cold and this approach emphasised quantity over quality.

Escoffier did away with this approach and replaced it with 'the Russian style'. Only one dish was served at a time, perfectly prepared, heated and proportioned for the diner. A sorbet was served after a strongly flavoured course to refresh the palate. The Frenchman created many new, lighter dishes with unusual and distinctive flavours.

Escoffier introduced new methods and practices for the kitchens. The food was freshly acquired each morning. The numerous kitchen staff were organised in disciplines, each responsible for a particular type of food. He forbade swearing, smoking, gambling and bullying amongst the staff. The traditional problem with cooks was consumption of alcohol, so he banned it and supplied cold barley water for them to drink instead.

Esscoffier always dressed very smartly and he insisted that the staff do the same, with white hats and jackets and highly polished shoes. He supervised all proceedings from his glass-fronted office.

The Savoy Hotel quickly garnered a reputation for exquisite cuisine and it attracted the rich, famous and glamorous. It was a favourite haunt of the nobility, politicians and actors. The great Australian soprano, Nellie Melba, performed in London and she sent Escoffier two tickets for the opera. When she came to dine at the Savoy, Escoffier presented her with a new creation – peach melba.

After leaving the Savoy in 1898, Escoffier went on to manage the restaurants at the Paris Ritz and London Carlton hotels. Escoffier created many new recipes and sauces and published a highly influential book, *Le Guide Culinaire*, which is still used today as a reference work. More importantly, his fresh approaches to kitchen management were adopted by hotels and restaurants throughout the world. He retired in 1920 and died in 1935.

INSIGHTS FOR INNOVATORS

Rearrange the process. Very often, you can innovate by changing the sequence in which things are done. Escoffier did this by serving one dish at a time, perfectly prepared, rather than presenting all the food at once.

Demand the highest standards and you can charge the highest prices. Escoffier transformed the Savoy kitchens by setting and maintaining strict disciplines for work practices. He established and rigorously protected his reputation as the best and most creative chef.

Make yourself memorable and distinctive. Get a catch phrase. Escoffier was known as 'the king of chefs and the chef of kings'. Once his reputation was established, his success was assured. If you position yourself as different from the rest in some memorable way, then you can use that as a lever for competitive advantage.

DICK FOSBURY

(BORN 1947)

Athlete who pioneered the Fosbury Flop

The fans packed into the Olympic Stadium in Mexico City in 1968 saw something they had never seen before. An athlete competing in the men's high jump went over with his back to the bar. The man was a 21-year-old American, Dick Fosbury. He won the gold medal with a leap of 2.24 metres, a new Olympic record.

The conventional way to undertake a high jump until then was the straddle method (or western roll), where the athlete went over the high jump bar facing down. It involved a complex manoeuvre of lifting the legs individually over the bar. At high school, Fosbury had found this approach difficult and had started to experiment with other ways of performing a high jump. He used a leap of the imagination and asked, 'What if I turned around and went over with my back to the bar?'

Most schools and athletic clubs had a high jump landing pit made of wood chips and sawdust, which is fine for the straddle jump, but very dangerous if you try landing on your back. However, Fosbury's high school in Medford, Oregon was one of the first in the country to use a foam landing pit. This enabled the student to try out his outlandish idea.

Although his coaches tried to dissuade him, Fosbury practised and developed his new method. He learnt to sprint diagonally towards the bar, then curve and leap backwards in a parabola. This gave him a lower centre of gravity than conventional jumpers.

He soon began to perform well and win competitions, but many coaches and commentators derided his new approach. One newspaper labelled him the 'World's laziest high jumper' while another said he looked like 'a fish flopping in a boat'. And so the term 'Fosbury Flop' was coined.

After he won the Olympic gold medal, everything changed. His new method became the standard for high jumpers everywhere.

INSIGHTS FOR INNOVATORS

New technologies present great opportunities for innovations. Timing is vital. The introduction of foam landing pits enabled a complete rethink of the high jump technique, yet most athletes and coaches around the world were stuck in the traditional paradigm. It took a bold bound of imagination for Fosbury to realise that an innovative method was possible.

The more well-established the method, the greater the opportunity for innovation. Whenever a system has been in place for a long time, there is a good prospect of replacing or updating it with a fresh approach. Just because thousands or millions of people are doing it the conventional way does not mean that is the best way.

Try turning the whole thing around. Lateral thinkers deliberately try to approach a problem from a different direction. Instead of facing the bar, Fosbury turned his back to it. You cannot look in a new direction by staring harder in the same direction. You have to physically turn. As Fosbury did!

FLORENCE NIGHTINGALE

(1820 – 1910)

The 'Lady with the Lamp' – reformer
and founder of modern nursing

Florence Nightingale was born into a wealthy, upper-class English family. At the time, her parents were in Florence as part of a tour of Europe, and she was named after the place of her birth. She was taught at home by her father and became skilled in languages and mathematics. In 1837, Nightingale felt that God was calling her to do good work. She was interested in nursing, but her parents considered it to be inappropriate for a woman of her upbringing. She was expected to prepare to become a wife. Her parents found her several eminent suitors, but she rejected them all and, eventually, they let her follow her passion.

She studied nursing in Germany and, at the age of 33, she became superintendent of a hospital for gentlewomen in Harley Street. The following year (1853) the Crimean War started. Russia invaded Turkey. Britain and France, who were both worried about Russia's imperial ambitions, went to Turkey's aid and declared war on Russia. The British soldiers in the Crimea suffered terribly from cholera and malaria. Men were dying at an alarming rate and newspaper reports described the desperate situation. Sidney Herbert, the war minister, knew Nightingale, and asked her to oversee a team of nurses in the military hospitals. In November 1854, she arrived in Scutari in Turkey with a team of 38 volunteer nurses. She found appalling conditions in the barracks hospitals. She saw poor sanitation, ineffective sewers, little ventilation and a lack of equipment. Men were dying rapidly from cholera, dysentery and typhus. She was outspoken in her criticisms of the poor conditions.

Military officers strongly objected to this woman's intervention and her forthright views on the need to reform military hospitals. Army doctors saw her comments as an attack on their professionalism. She received little help or cooperation, so she contacted John Delane, the editor of *The Times*, and publicised the stories of how badly the soldiers were suffering in unsanitary conditions. The result was that she was given responsibility for organising the barracks hospitals. With her nurses, she rigorously improved the conditions and reduced the mortality rate for wounded soldiers from 42 per cent to 2 per cent.

During the Crimean campaign, Florence Nightingale gained the nickname 'The Lady with the Lamp', following a report in *The Times*:

> **'She is a ministering angel without any exaggeration in these hospitals. When all the medical officers have retired for the night and silence and darkness have settled down upon those miles of prostrate sick, she may be observed alone, with a little lamp in her hand, making her solitary rounds.'**

When she returned to England in 1856, Nightingale was a national heroine. She used this status to launch a campaign to improve the quality of nursing in military hospitals. She met Queen Victoria and Prince Albert and her efforts resulted in the formation of the Army Medical College.

She wrote two highly influential books, *Notes on Nursing* (1859) and *Notes on Hospitals* (1863). She raised money to improve the quality of nursing. In 1860, she used this money to found the Nightingale Home and Training School for Nurses at St Thomas's Hospital in London. She also became heavily involved in the training of nurses.

Nightingale held strong opinions on women's rights. She made a forceful case for the removal of restrictions that prevented women from having careers.

In later life, Nightingale suffered from poor health and, in 1895, she became blind. She died on 13 August 1910.

Nightingale's lasting legacy has been her role in founding the modern nursing profession. She set a wonderful example for nurses everywhere of compassion and commitment to patient care. Her policies on hospital sanitation and organisation influenced military and civilian hospital practice and have saved countless lives.

If you see something that desperately needs to be changed, then change it. Lead the process with your personal action. Florence Nightingale took charge to transform nursing care for soldiers. It was her personal intervention that led the change.

Use contacts and the media to overcome vested interests who oppose innovation. High ranking officials resented Nightingale's interference. Nightingale published reports in *The Times* to expose and bypass their objections. If you face a challenge, think about who you know who could help.

DID YOU KNOW?... Florence Nightingale was one of the first people to use pie charts to convey statistical information. She used statistics to analyse diseases and to make the case for reforms in sanitation. She was a fine mathematician and, in 1859, she became the first female member of the Royal Statistical Society.

On 12 December 1901, Marconi amazed the world when he sent and received the first wireless message across the Atlantic Ocean, from Cornwall, England, to Newfoundland, Canada.

Guglielmo Marconi was born the son of an Italian aristocrat and an Irishwoman, Annie Jameson, from the whiskey family. The boy showed a keen interest in science and, in particular, in sending electrical signals. In 1894, he sent a signal a short distance and, a year later, he sent one more than a mile. He showed his discovery to the Italian Ministry of Post and Telegraphs, who evinced no interest because they believed that the telegraph could already send signals long distances over wires. So, the young Marconi set off for England, the world's premier maritime power, where he believed his big ideas might be better received. He was right.

In 1896, he sent a signal a mile across London. The next year, he received his first patent. In 1899, he sent signals across the English Channel and, in the same year, he founded the London-based Marconi Telegraph Company. However, most experts of the day believed that radio signals could travel only over a line-of-sight distance and that the curvature of the Earth would prevent the long-distance use of radio. Marconi set up his famous experiment with the most powerful radio transmitter then built in Poldhu, Cornwall. Marconi and his assistant, George Kemp, set up a radio receiver in Newfoundland with an aerial consisting of 500 feet of wire supported by kites. They waited three days before the signal – a Morse Code S – was received. The news that radio waves had crossed the Atlantic was sensational. Many disbelieved it. How could it be possible? What the experts (and Marconi) did not know was that there was a charged layer around the Earth called the ionosphere that could reflect radio waves.

Within a year, Marconi set up dependable radio communication with ships over 2,000 miles away. Eventually, the Marconi Company linked the entire British Empire by radio.

In 1909, Marconi and Karl Braun were awarded the Nobel Prize in Physics 'in recognition of their contributions to the development of wireless telegraphy'. When Marconi died in Rome in 1937, radio stations the world over went silent for two minutes in tribute to the great pioneer.

INSIGHTS FOR INNOVATORS

Innovators do not trust experts. They do not trust theories, models or spreadsheets. They trust real-life experiments. Marconi ignored all the authorities who declared that long-distance radio signal transmission was impossible. He tried it and it worked.

Be a showman. Marconi did not undertake just longer and slightly longer distances. He went for a massive distance of over 2,000 miles, knowing that if he succeeded it would stun opinion around the world. It was a bold and risky move, but it paid off.

Go to where your ideas will be welcomed. Marconi found little appreciation for his innovative telegraphy concepts in Italy, so he moved to Great Britain, which, at that time, was a technology leader. Move to where the action is in your speciality.

GUSTAVE EIFFEL

(1832 – 1923)

Builder of the Eiffel Tower

In 1889, France held a Centennial Exposition to commemorate the French Revolution. A competition was held for a suitable monument. Over 100 plans were submitted. The one that was chosen was that of an eminent bridge engineer, Gustave Eiffel. He proposed a 300 metre (984 feet) tower of a lattice design in wrought iron. It was an audacious plan that was met with amazement, scepticism and outright opposition. Nothing remotely like it had ever been constructed. It was twice as high as the next highest building in the world. It would dominate the Parisian landscape.

A 'Committee of Three Hundred' was formed (one member for each metre of the tower's height) to oppose the plan. It included some of the most prominent and influential people in French artistic society, including Guy de Maupassant, Charles Gounod and Jules Massenet. They petitioned the government and the national press. They said, 'Imagine for a moment a giddy, ridiculous tower dominating Paris like a gigantic black smokestack, crushing under its barbaric bulk Notre Dame, the Tour de Saint-Jacques, the Louvre, the Dome of les Invalides, the Arc de Triomphe, all of our humiliated monuments will disappear in this ghastly dream. And for twenty years ... we shall see stretching like a blot of ink the hateful shadow of the hateful column of bolted sheet metal.'

However, Eiffel had powerful allies and he fought back by comparing his tower to the Egyptian pyramids. He appealed to French national pride saying, 'My tower will be the tallest edifice ever erected by man. Will it not also be grandiose in its way?' The tower was built in a matter of months. It remained the tallest building in the world until the completion of the Chrysler Building in New York in 1930. It became one of the world's most popular tourist attractions and a symbol of Paris around the globe.

Gustave Eiffel graduated from the prestigious École Centrale des Arts et Manufactures in 1855. As an architect and civil engineer, he specialised in metal construction, especially in bridges. In 1877, he constructed a bridge over the Douro River in Portugal with a 160 metre (525 foot) steel arch. It was the greatest arch span anywhere at the time. But he soon exceeded it with the Garabit Viaduct in southern France, which, at 120 metres (400 feet) above the river, was for many years the highest bridge in the world. He was always ambitious to create works that were longer, taller or bigger than those elsewhere.

Eiffel designed many bridges and railway stations around the world. He employed innovative techniques and was one of the first civil engineers to use compressed air caissons and hollow cast-iron piers in bridge building. His design for the movable dome of the observatory at Nice was particularly inventive. He also designed the framework for the Statue of Liberty, which was given by France to the people of the USA.

In later life, he studied and made important contributions in aerodynamics and meteorology. He founded the world's first aerodynamics laboratory near Paris. He died in his home in Paris in 1923.

Eiffel's work was highly influential for a number of reasons. He set ambitious new standards for metal construction, using innovative designs and methods. He was also a pioneer in his approach to engineering work. He insisted on detailed calculations of all forces involved, together with high specifications of accuracy in drawing and manufacture. He designed two of the most iconic buildings of the nineteenth century – the Statue of Liberty and the Eiffel Tower. He showed that metal structures could be beautiful, durable and strong. His remarkable constructions and, in particular, the Eiffel Tower earned him the nickname, 'the magician of iron'.

INSIGHTS FOR INNOVATORS

The greater the innovation, the greater the opposition. Eiffel's daring plan for the world's tallest tower in Paris provoked fierce criticism from those who said it was not feasible and from those who said it was too ugly. He calmly faced down his critics and lobbied hard for his plan, appealing to the vision and pride of the French Government and people.

Combine precision and creativity. Eiffel's designs and methods were highly innovative, but he did not sacrifice accuracy or quality in the design detail or in construction. His products were ground-breaking, artistic and reliable.

DID YOU KNOW ?... The Eiffel Tower is the most visited paid monument in the world with around seven million visitors every year.

HEDY LAMARR

(1914 – 2000)

Actress and inventor

Hedwig Eva Maria Kiesler was born in 1914, in Vienna, Austria. Her father was a banker and her mother a pianist. She became an actress and, in 1933, at the age of 18, she starred in the Czech film *Ecstasy*, by Gustav Machaty. It became notorious because of its sexual themes.

Also, at the age of 18, Hedwig married Friedrich Mandl, a prosperous Austrian arms maker. He supplied equipment to the fascist governments of Germany and Italy and had received Hitler and Mussolini in his home. She accompanied him to meetings and conferences and gained an interest in science and technology. Her marriage was unhappy; her husband was controlling and jealous. To escape, she changed clothes with her maid and, in disguise, fled to Paris. There she met the film magnate Louis Mayer, who recruited her for Hollywood and persuaded her to change her name to Hedy Lamarr. He promoted her in the USA as the 'world's most beautiful woman'.

She became an immediate box-office sensation after the release of her first American film, *Algiers*, opposite Charles Boyer. Her exotic raven-haired beauty made her a film idol. She starred in *Lady of the Tropics* (1939) with Robert Taylor; *Boom Town* (1940) with Clark Gable, *Tortilla Flat* (1942) with Spencer Tracy; and *Samson and Delilah* (1949) with Victor Mature. She made 18 films in the 1940s, but her career faded in the 1950s. She became bored with acting.

She had always had an interest in technology and invention. She created a design for a better traffic stoplight and made a tablet that dissolved in water to produce a fizzy drink. In 1942, during the prime of her film career, Lamarr and a colleague, the composer George Antheil, received a patent for a radio signalling system. In an attempt to help the war effort, they developed a better way to guide torpedoes. It used 'frequency hopping' (or spread spectrum) to prevent the enemy jamming the signal. The US Navy did not adopt the technology during the war but, eventually, took it up in the 1960s. However, key elements of their work are now built into modern cell phones, Wi-Fi and Bluetooth technology. By the time of its widespread use, the patent on spread spectrum had expired, but it led, in 2014, to Lamarr and Antheil being inducted into the National Inventors Hall of Fame. In 1997, Lamarr became the first woman to receive the prestigious BULBIE Gnass Spirit of Achievement Award.

Lamarr was married six times. She became a recluse in her old age and died in Florida in 2000.

INSIGHTS FOR INNOVATORS

Having a successful career does not stop you from being an inventor or innovator in another field. Hedy Lamarr was at the height of her acting success when she devoted her spare time to inventing. She was known worldwide for her glamour, beauty and acting. Most people would have settled for that. But she wanted to make a big contribution to the war effort. She took a big challenge and, together with her colleague, came up with an invention that is in everyday use over 70 years later.

Recognition and reward can be a long time coming. We have seen this with other innovators. It took a long time for the full benefit of Lamarr's innovation to be realised. If you want instant gratification, then do not become an inventor. You have to be committed to the challenge for its own sake.

Do not judge a book by its cover. Lamarr shattered the stereotype of the glamorous Hollywood actress by becoming a successful scientific inventor. She did not conform to the pattern. She created her own.

DID YOU KNOW?... In an oblique tribute to the actress, Mel Brooks included in his 1974 film *Blazing Saddles* a leading character called Hedley Lamarr, played by Harvey Korman.

MUHAMMAD YUNUS

(BORN 1940)

Bangladeshi founder of the Grameen Bank, pioneer of microcredit and Nobel Prize winner

Muhammad Yunus was born the son of a goldsmith in a village in Chittagong in modern-day Bangladesh. He was the third of fourteen children, five of whom died as infants. He was inspired by his mother who was always keen to help poor people in their town. The boy grew up wanting to help eradicate poverty. He studied Economics at Dhaka University and then worked as a research assistant in the national Bureau of Economics. He became a university lecturer. In 1965, he gained a Fulbright Scholarship to study at the Vanderbilt University in the USA, where he gained a PhD in Economics. After lecturing in the USA, he returned to Bangladesh, where he became head of Economics at Chittagong University.

In 1974, he led a group of his students on a field trip to a poor village. They met a woman who made bamboo stools. She had to borrow the equivalent of 20 US cents to buy the bamboo for each stool made. She borrowed money from local loan agents, who charged exorbitant interest rates and so she remained in poverty.

Yunus tried an experiment. Using his own funds, he made a loan of $27 to a group of 42 women basket-weavers. He found that even this small amount made a huge difference and enabled them to build their small enterprises and, eventually, to pay it back.

He started to issue many more microloans in the face of obstruction and criticism from banks and the government for whom the idea was too revolutionary. In 1983, he founded the Grameen Bank, meaning village bank, to make microloans to poor entrepreneurs. Yunus met strong opposition from anti-capitalist radicals and from conservative imams, who warned women that they would be denied a Muslim burial, if they borrowed money from Grameen. But the Bank proved very popular and made millions of small loans. Grameen fostered an innovative system of 'solidarity groups' of people who band together to apply for loans and who act as co-guarantors of repayment. Their joint informal commitment helps them to build successful businesses and to pay back the debt.

In Bangladesh, Grameen grew to over 2,500 branches, lending small amounts to over 8 million borrowers in 80,000 villages. Ninety-five per cent of the borrowers are women and the default rate on the loans is less than 3 per cent, which is better than most conventional banks. The success of the Grameen microfinance model has been copied in over 100 countries around the world.

In 2006, Yunus was awarded the Nobel Peace Prize, along with Grameen Bank, for their efforts to create economic and social development. The Nobel Committee said, 'Muhammad Yunus has shown himself to be a leader who has managed to translate visions into practical action for the benefit of millions of people, not only in Bangladesh, but also in many other countries. Loans to poor people without any financial security had appeared to be an impossible idea. From modest beginnings three decades ago, Yunus has, first and foremost through Grameen Bank, developed microcredit into an ever more important instrument in the struggle against poverty.'

Yunus was the first Bangladeshi to receive a Nobel Prize. He announced that he would donate the $1.4 million award to create a company to provide low-cost food for the poor and to build an eye hospital for the poor in Bangladesh.

INSIGHTS FOR INNOVATORS

Innovate with a moral purpose. Muhammad Yunus had a strong desire to help poor people. He applied his knowledge of economics and finance to come up with an innovative model of tiny loans to groups of poor entrepreneurs. He found a new way to alleviate poverty by empowering women who wanted to run their own businesses and work their way up. Your ethics can drive your innovations; see Anita Roddick for another example of this theme.

Innovate by minimisation. Most banks would make only larger loans because of the administration involved. They also require some form of collateral guarantee. Yunus cut the paperwork to a minimum, did away with collateral and made tiny loans that other banks would laugh at. He found that the solidarity of groups led to a strong shared commitment to pay back. Can you find a tiny solution to a problem that bypasses big, clumsy or bureaucratic conventions?

DID YOU KNOW?... The great success of Muhammad Yunus generated envy and resentment. After he criticised state corruption, in 2001, the Bangladesh Government launched an investigation of the Grameen Bank and ordered his removal as managing director.

TRAVIS KALANICK

(BORN 1976)

Entrepreneur and founder of Uber

Travis Kalanick was born in Los Angeles. He enrolled at the University of California, Los Angeles (UCLA), to study Computer Engineering but, in 1998, he and some colleagues dropped out of UCLA to found Scour Inc. The company developed a multimedia search engine and a peer-to-peer file-sharing service. In 2000, some of the largest media companies in the USA issued a lawsuit against Scour, alleging copyright infringement and the company filed for bankruptcy.

In 2001, Kalanick started a new company, Red Swoosh, which offered peer-to-peer file-sharing. It was acquired by Akamai Technologies for $19 million in 2007.

In 2009, Kalanick and Garrett Camp founded Uber, a mobile application that connects passengers with drivers of vehicles for hire and ridesharing services. The company started as a two-car operation in San Francisco and then rocketed upwards. By 2016, it had over 1 million drivers, was delivering over 3 million rides a day in 66 countries, and was valued at $62 billion. It is claimed to be the fastest-growing start-up in business history. So big was the impact, that Uber became a verb meaning to disrupt an entire industry model. It became the leading exponent of the 'gig economy', which allows people to make money by sharing their resources. It includes many other companies, such as Airbnb and TaskRabbit.

Uber has run into fierce opposition from taxi companies and trade unions around the world because of its disruptive effect and novel labour model. Kalanick has been pugnacious in his response and is quite happy to take on vested interests. He said, 'There are a lot of rules in cities that were designed to protect a particular incumbent, but not to move a city's constituents, a city's citizens, and the city itself, forward. And that's a problem.'

He went on to say, 'New York had the same number of taxi licenses for 60 years. The cab owners lobbied together and created artificial scarcity. Things got so bad that nobody else could get into the business. A driver had to pay almost $150 dollars a day to get a license and drive a cab.' He claims that Uber empowers drivers, delivers value to passengers and reduces congestion.

INSIGHTS FOR INNOVATORS

Innovate with other people's resources, especially if they are under-utilised resources. Uber does not own any cars. It is, fundamentally, an app that links people who want rides with people who are prepared to provide them. How can you harness the 'gig economy' to help other people provide a service that customers will value?

Find something broken and fix it. Kalanick had the idea for Uber when he was in Paris in 2009 and could not get a taxi. Most people would just complain or take the bus, but Kalanick thought there must be a better way. He thought, 'Why not harness the capacity of all the drivers in Paris who would be happy to give me a ride for a fee?' Wherever there is a constraint on a supply there is an opportunity for an innovator to find a new way to meet the demand.

Your big win is unlikely to be the first company you start. Uber is Kalanick's third internet start-up. His first went bankrupt and his second was a small success (compared with Uber). Many entrepreneurs find that their first few ventures are learning experiences and the big payback comes later. Do not be downhearted if you have some failures.

PART 7
SCIENTIST

SIR ALEXANDER FLEMING

(1881 – 1955)

The doctor who discovered penicillin

O n 3 September 1928, Scottish doctor and bacteriologist Alexander Fleming returned from holiday to his laboratory. He sorted through a large stack of petri dishes that had accumulated before he had gone away. He noticed that one contained a mould that had killed the bacteria in the dish. In other dishes, the bacteria continued to thrive. 'That's funny,' he thought. He investigated the mould carefully and grew it in a pure culture. He found that it killed a number of bacteria that caused diseases. He called it penicillin. It was the first antibiotic and would transform the treatment of infections and save countless millions of lives. He later said, 'When I woke up just after dawn on September 28, 1928, I certainly didn't plan to revolutionise all medicine by discovering the world's first antibiotic, or bacteria killer. But I suppose that was exactly what I did.'

Fleming was born in 1881 in Ayrshire, the son of a farmer. He moved to London at the age of 13 and trained as a doctor. He qualified with distinction in 1906 and began research at St Mary's Hospital Medical School at the University of London. In 1908, he won the gold medal as the top medical student. In the First World War, Fleming served in the Army Medical Corps and was mentioned in dispatches. He worked as a bacteriologist, studying wound infections. After the war, he returned to St Mary's.

Fleming published his discovery in 1929, in the *British Journal of Experimental Pathology*, but no one seemed to notice. Through the 1930s, he continued to experiment with penicillin, but found that it was difficult to cultivate in any quantity. Eventually, Australian Howard Florey and Ernst Chain (a refugee from the Nazis in Germany) at the Radcliffe Infirmary in Oxford found a way to mass-produce the antibiotic and it was used widely to save the lives of wounded servicemen in the Second World War.

Fleming wrote many papers on bacteriology, immunology and chemotherapy. He became a professor at the University of

London. He was knighted in 1944. In 1945, Fleming, Florey and Chain shared the Nobel Prize in Medicine. Fleming died of a heart attack in 1955.

INSIGHTS FOR INNOVATORS

Welcome the unexpected. Most people would have cleared out all the old petri dishes and ignored a strange mouldy fungus. But Fleming was curious. He seized the serendipitous moment and investigated the unusual occurrence. Great innovators are always inquisitive and see unexpected results as opportunities for learning and discovery.

You cannot do it all on your own. Fleming needed the help of Florey and Chain to turn his discovery into something that could be used for large-scale treatment of diseases. Together, their work has saved millions of lives. Before antibiotics, small infections could lead to amputations or death. Fleming did not keep his discovery to himself. He published it and worked with others to change the world.

Do not be too tidy! Being messy can sometimes help. If Fleming had cleaned all his equipment before leaving for holiday, he would not have discovered penicillin. If everything in your office is neat and tidy, that helps you find things, but you might lose out on the random associations that can sometimes trigger great ideas.

ALEXANDER GRAHAM BELL

(1847 – 1922)

Inventor of the telephone

Alexander Graham Bell was responsible for many ground-breaking discoveries, including most notably the invention of the telephone. He made significant improvements in communication for the deaf. He was born in Edinburgh, Scotland, where he attended university. His father was a teacher of elocution and his mother, despite being very deaf, was an accomplished pianist. The young boy would press his mouth close to his mother's forehead so that she could feel the vibration of his words.

He taught at his father's school for the deaf in London before emigrating to North America in 1870. Two years later, he opened a school in Boston to train teachers of those with impaired hearing.

Bell dreamt of inventing a machine that would help the deaf to hear. He experimented with the vibrations and transmission of sound. He was assisted by a skilled electrician, Thomas Watson. Bell eventually found that he could transmit sounds using electric currents. Speech waves caused a diaphragm to vibrate and this varied the current flowing in wires attached to the instrument. The US Patent Office issued a patent in Bell's name for the telephone on 7 March 1876. Three days later, the invention worked. Bell knocked over a flask of fluid and shouted into the device, 'Mr Watson, come here. I want you!' Watson heard the words. It was the world's first telephone call.

Bell carried out a series of public demonstrations and lectures to introduce the telephone to the public and to the scientific community. People were amazed when they heard live voices from far away. The Bell Telephone Company was founded in 1877. In the same year, Bell married Mabel Hubbard, a deaf woman who had been a pupil at his school. In due course, the popularity of the telephone exploded. His engineers added a microphone, one of Thomas Edison's inventions, which meant that there was no longer any need to shout into the telephone in order to be heard. By 1886, more than 150,000 people in the USA owned telephones.

Other individuals and companies had worked on ideas like the telephone, but Bell pipped them to the post. His success spurred resentment. The Bell Company faced over 580 court challenges concerning patents for the invention. Five went to the US Supreme Court. None was successful.

Bell was a great believer in experimentation. He always wanted to leave the beaten path. He said, 'We should not keep forever on the public road, going only where others have gone; we should leave the beaten track occasionally and enter the woods. Every time you do that you will be certain to find something that you have never seen before.'

Bell carried out important research in other technical fields including optical telecommunications, hydrofoils and aeronautics. He held 18 patents when he died in 1922. After his death, the entire telephone system throughout North America was shut down for one minute in tribute to the man.

INSIGHTS FOR INNOVATORS

Copy an idea from nature. Bell studied deafness and the workings of the human ear. The diaphragm in the telephone was based on the diaphragm in the human ear. Many other great innovations and designs have their basis in the workings of nature.

Big companies can miss opportunities. At an early stage, Bell and his partners offered to sell the telephone patent outright to the large telegraph company Western Union for $100,000. Western Union declined because they saw little commercial potential in the invention. Two years later, the president of Western Union, admitting his mistake, said that the patent was worth $25 million but, by then, the Bell Company no longer wanted to sell.

If you have a truly great and original innovation, then patent it. The cost and effort are considerable, but it is sometimes the best way to protect your intellectual property – especially if it is a specific and novel technical solution. In other cases, keeping a trade secret (e.g. the formula for Coca-Cola) or simply speed to market are better options.

ARCHIMEDES

(287 – 212 BC)

Mathematician, inventor and engineer

Archimedes was the greatest mathematician of the ancient world and one of the greatest of all time. He was born in Syracuse in Sicily and educated in Alexandria in Egypt. He returned to Syracuse, where he devoted his life to mathematics, physics, astronomy, engineering and invention.

He once observed children playing on a seesaw consisting of a plank of wood and a big stone. If the children did not balance, then they moved the plank along the stone until they did. He pondered the implications of this and worked out a simple formula for a lever, showing the longer the lever the greater the load that it could move. He famously said, 'Give me a place to stand and a lever large enough and I will lift the Earth.'

The most celebrated story about Archimedes concerns the King of Syracuse, Hieron. A goldsmith had made the king a crown and claimed that it was solid gold. The king thought it might be a mixture of gold and other metals, so he asked Archimedes if he could determine whether the crown was pure gold, without damaging it. Archimedes contemplated this tricky problem for many days without making much progress. Inspiration struck when he sat in his bath. He realised that, if he immersed the crown in a full container of water, it would displace its exact volume of water from the container. Once he knew the volume and weight of the crown, he could calculate its density and compare that with the known density of gold. He did so and proved that the crown was adulterated with silver. The great man went on to postulate the Archimedes principle that a body immersed in a fluid loses weight equal to the weight of the fluid displaced. The story goes that Archimedes was so thrilled with his discovery that he leapt from his bath and ran naked down the road shouting 'Eureka!', the Greek word for 'I have found it'.

In mechanics, in addition to defining the principle of the lever, he is credited with inventing the compound pulley and a hydraulic screw for raising water from a lower to a higher level.

In mathematics, he proved important geometrical theorems, such as the area of a circle, the surface area and volume of a sphere, and the area under a parabola. He calculated an accurate approximation of pi, defined the spiral bearing his name, and created a system using exponents for expressing very large numbers. He even anticipated modern calculus by developing concepts of infinitesimals.

During the Roman conquest of Sicily in 214 BC, Archimedes worked for the state, and was attributed with developing a giant catapult and a mirror system for focusing the sun's rays on the invaders' boats and igniting them. After Syracuse was captured, Archimedes was killed by a Roman soldier. It is said that he was so absorbed in his calculations, he told his killer not to disturb him.

INSIGHTS FOR INNOVATORS

A flash of inspiration often comes when you relax. There are many instances where great thinkers were puzzled by a problem and, then, when they did something else, the solution came to them. When your brain switches into a different mode, it can sometimes turn up a great idea. This is what happened to Archimedes in his bath. When you are stumped by a difficult challenge, let it incubate, go for a walk or take a bath.

When you have a Eureka moment, capture it. Write down your great idea and then test it. Turn theory into practice with an experiment.

A lever is a great metaphor for an innovation. Archimedes developed the principle of the lever as something that could move the Earth. What can you come up with that makes life easier for people? How can you get a bigger result for a small effort?

CHARLES DARWIN

(1809 – 1882)

Naturalist who expounded
the theory of evolution

Charles Darwin was born in Shrewsbury in England. His grandfather was Erasmus Darwin, a renowned doctor, scientist and poet. His father was a doctor who wanted Charles to become either a doctor or a clergyman and he was disappointed when his son chose a career in natural science. Darwin graduated from Cambridge University whereon his botany professor John Henslow suggested that he take a position as the official naturalist aboard HMS *Beagle*, a ship that was due to take a five-year scientific survey trip around the world. Although he was at first reluctant to spend five years on the tiny vessel, Darwin agreed and the journey proved to be the turning point in the life of the brilliant young naturalist. The 90 ft ship, commanded by Captain Robert Fitzroy, set sail in 1831.

On the voyage, Darwin studied thousands of plants, animals and fossils around the world. He was particularly fascinated by the wildlife on the Galapagos Islands, which proved to be a real-life laboratory. He noticed that finches (and other animals) on different islands had different characteristics and he deduced that they were all descended from a common ancestor finch, but they had developed separately. He conceived his theory that species survive through a process of 'natural selection'. Those species that successfully adapted to meet the exigencies of their habitat survived, whilst less successful variations died off.

At the time, people believed that all species came into being at the start of the world or were created over time. In either case, the species were believed to remain the same. Darwin knew that his theory of the evolution of species would be heretical and incendiary. He waited 20 years and gathered a tremendous amount of scientific evidence before publishing his findings in his classic book, *The Origin of Species*, in 1859. His decision was triggered partly by the publication of a similar idea by fellow naturalist Alfred Wallace.

The book was a sensation in the scientific community and caused inspiration and indignation across the world. Darwin was mocked and ridiculed – particularly for his notion that humans and apes were descended from a common ancestor. But many eminent thinkers came to his support and the theory is now widely accepted today as one of the most brilliant ideas of the scientific enlightenment. Darwin is considered to be one of the most influential figures in human history. He was honoured by burial in Westminster Abbey in London.

INSIGHTS FOR INNOVATORS

Bide your time. Often, an innovator will rush to market with his or her new idea, but sometimes the world is not yet ready. Darwin knew that his radical theory of evolution would shake society and provoke a strong reaction. He strengthened his scientific standing and gathered a wealth of irrefutable data. He discussed his findings with a handful of trusted colleagues. Eventually, he published his book and unleashed his shattering idea on the world.

Be prepared for the reaction. Darwin was castigated and lampooned up and down the country. People could not accept that they were descended from an ape-like ancestor. Although he suffered criticism and ill-health, Darwin continued to work, investigate and write for the final 20 years of his life. In 1871, he published *The Descent of Man, and Selection in Relation to Sex*, which applied evolutionary theory to human evolution.

Lobby the key opinion leaders. Darwin knew that there would be opposition in the popular media to his ground-breaking theory, so he corresponded deliberately with leading scientists over several years to convince them

▶

to support his approach. He even kept a list of those for and against his proposition. At the time of publication, he could call on many eminent allies to come to his support against poorly informed attacks. He did not have to do all the defence work himself. To promote your radical idea, do not try to persuade the whole world. Focus on the most influential thought leaders in your field.

DMITRI MENDELEEV

(1834 – 1907)

Russian chemist who created
the periodic table of elements

Dmitri Mendeleev was born one of fifteen children (the exact number is uncertain) in Tobolsk, Siberia in 1834. His father, Ivan, was a teacher who became blind and lost his teaching post. His mother, Maria, was obliged to work as the manager of a glass factory to support herself and her children. The factory burned down in 1848 and the recently widowed Maria took her impoverished family on a long journey across Russia to St Petersburg. Young Dmitri proved to be an excellent student. After graduation, he contracted tuberculosis and had to move south to the better climate of the Crimea, where he taught chemistry. When his health recovered, he went to study at the University of Heidelberg in Germany.

Mendeleev returned to teach at the University of St Petersburg, which was where he achieved his great breakthrough. He loved card games. He wrote the weight for each element on a separate index card and then laid them out as if he was playing a game of solitaire. He realised that elements with similar properties could be arranged in a 'suit', ordered by atomic weight. He arranged all the known elements by atomic weight into a table and showed it as a picture. Using this method, he could predict undiscovered elements from the gaps in the table. In 1869, he presented his periodic law and table of the elements to the Russian Chemical Society. His ideas were met initially with scepticism, but the discovery of new elements, which fitted his patterns, led to their acceptance in the scientific community.

In addition to his discoveries in theoretical chemistry, Mendeleev made important contributions in the use of petroleum, in the coal industry and in agricultural methods. He became director of the Russian Board of Weights and Measures.

INSIGHTS FOR INNOVATORS

Draw a picture of your problem in order to view it in a new way. By laying out the elements like a suit of cards, Mendeleev observed recurring patterns in the chemical and physical properties of different groups of elements. How could you use a diagram, picture or flowchart to represent your issue? Sometimes, looking at something in graphical form helps give you the insight you need.

Look for a pattern and use it to predict results. The ultimate test for Mendeleev's theory was that, with it, he could forecast where new elements would be found to fit the pattern. He predicted existence and atomic weights of Gallium, Scandium and Germanium. When they were discovered, he was vindicated. Use real-life experiments to test your innovative idea.

Take the existing order and deliberately rearrange it. Ray Kroc did it with restaurants, Govindappa Venkataswamy did it with cataract operations and Mendeleev did it with the periodic table.

DID YOU KNOW ?... At Mendeleev's funeral in St Petersburg in 1907, students carried a large copy of the periodic table of the elements in honour of his work.

EDWARD JENNER

(1749 – 1823)

Doctor who discovered the
smallpox vaccine

Edward Jenner was an English country doctor who pioneered the smallpox vaccine, the world's first vaccine. He is called 'the father of immunology', and his work is said to have saved more lives than the work of any other human.

He was born the eighth of nine children. His father was a vicar in a village in Gloucestershire. Edward was an able student. He studied surgery and anatomy under the eminent surgeon John Hunter at St George's Hospital in London. Hunter gave Jenner a powerful piece of advice – 'Don't think; try.'

Returning to his native countryside in 1773, Jenner became a successful family doctor and surgeon, practising in the village of Berkeley.

At that time, smallpox was a curse on humanity. It is estimated that some 60 per cent of the population caught the disease and a third of those died of it.

Jenner was fascinated by an unusual fact that had been known for some time; milkmaids hardly ever caught smallpox. He asked himself why this might be. His hypothesis was that they caught cowpox from cows and that this somehow protected them from catching smallpox. Cowpox was similar to smallpox, but much less virulent.

In 1796, Jenner tested his theory by injecting an eight-year-old boy, James Phipps, with cowpox pus. The boy developed cowpox. Jenner subsequently introduced smallpox infected material to the boy, who proved to be immune to the disease.

Jenner carried out further tests on different subjects and showed rigorously that cowpox pus could be used to protect people from smallpox. He described his experiment in a paper for the Royal Society in 1797. The reaction was sceptical, with more proof demanded. Jenner repeated the experiment on several other children, including his own son. In 1798, the results were published and Jenner recommended mass vaccination. His proposals were ridiculed. People considered it outrageous that a person should be inoculated with material from a diseased animal.

Eventually, the medical authorities were convinced by the evidence and starting vaccination programmes. The practice spread first in Europe and then across the world, with countless lives saved. In 1979, the World Health Organization declared that smallpox had been eradicated.

Jenner became famous and devoted his energies to medical research and developing the process of vaccination. He died in 1823.

INSIGHTS FOR INNOVATORS

Ask searching questions. Jenner famously asked, 'Why do milkmaids never catch smallpox?' Others had observed this anomaly, but he kept asking and used the question as a starting point for his brilliant concept. Instead of asking why something happens, try asking why it does not happen. A different question leads to a different answer and a different idea.

'Don't think; try' – is a provocative precept for innovators. Of course, we must think but we must not become paralysed by cogitation. We need to experiment to discover the remarkable. Jenner's approach appears dangerous and rustic compared with modern medical procedures. But it was only with evidence that he could convince people to change their ways. Theories are not as powerful as empirical data when it comes to changing minds. Prove your innovation with your experiments.

DID YOU KNOW?... The word vaccine was coined by Edward Jenner. It comes from the Latin word *vacca*, a cow.

EDWIN LAND

(1909 – 1991)

Chemist who invented
the Polaroid camera

Edwin Land was a US inventor who had studied chemistry. In 1943, on holiday in Santa Fe, he took a photograph of his three-year-old daughter Jennifer. She asked why she could not see the result straight away and she kept asking why. Land pondered this question and an idea formed in his mind. He went on to develop the Polaroid camera, a revolutionary product that sold over 150 million units and made Land into a celebrity. His daughter's naive question had led him to challenge the assumptions that the whole photography industry took for granted.

Land was born in 1909, in Bridgeport, Connecticut. He attended Harvard University for a year, studying chemistry, but dropped out and moved to New York where he continued to experiment. During the day, he studied at the New York Public Library and, at night, he conducted research independently at a Columbia University laboratory. As a result, he developed a remarkable advance in polarising light technology, which he called the Polaroid J sheet. In 1937, he co-founded the Polaroid Corporation to develop his ideas.

Polaroid technology found many practical applications, including in sunglasses and night-vision goggles. During the war, Land's company developed a method to reveal enemy camouflage and it went on to design systems for the U2 spy plane. But its biggest success was the Polaroid camera, which proved very popular. It stayed on the market for 50 years.

At work, Land was known for his diligence, his long hours in the lab and his progressive management policies. He hired women and minorities for research and management positions at a time when they were more likely to be offered secretarial or clerical roles. He carried out major research in the fields of optics, light, photography, colour perception and sight. He held hundreds of patents. He had been too busy to complete his studies at Harvard but, in 1957, the University awarded him an honorary doctorate for his lifetime of scientific achievement.

Challenge assumptions by asking searching questions. At work, we tend to ask one or two questions and then plunge into ideas and discussion. But, by asking more questions, and more basic, even childlike questions, we can discover insights that challenge our assumptions and allow us to reach deeper issues and better solutions. Edwin Land did this and went on to find a radically different and faster way to produce photographs.

Reach for the unattainable star. Land said this: 'Don't undertake a project unless it is manifestly important and nearly impossible.' Great innovators tackle problems that others consider too difficult or too risky.

Why should customers wait? If people suffer any inconvenience in service, then there is an opportunity for an innovator to offer an improvement. Land's daughter expressed a need that many customers had, but did not express. Why do we have to wait? Find the source of customer difficulty and you have found a starting point for innovation.

GALILEO

(1564 – 1642)

The father of modern science

G alileo Galilei is recognised as one of the greatest astronomers, physicists and mathematicians. He was the first person to examine the night sky using a telescope and so founded modern astronomy. He demonstrated that nature followed mathematical principles and he developed the foundations of mechanics. He is considered to be the father of modern science.

He was born in Pisa in Italy in 1564. His father Vincenzo, a well-known musician, decided that his son should become a doctor, so he was sent to the University of Pisa to study medicine. The story goes that, as a student, sitting in the Cathedral of Pisa, he observed a hanging lamp swinging to and fro. He noticed that each swing took the same time, regardless of how great the swing. Therefore, he deduced that a pendulum could be used to measure time. Fascinated by the mathematics of this, he persuaded his father that he should give up medicine and devote his studies to mathematics.

Galileo had a remarkable talent for mathematics. He went on to become professor of mathematics at the University of Pisa. In 1604, he proved that all objects fall at the same rate, regardless of their weight, contradicting the popular belief that heavier objects fell faster. One of his most important new ideas was that you could test theories by conducting experiments. For example, he showed that one could test theories about falling bodies using an inclined plane to slow down the rate of descent.

In 1609, Galileo learned of the invention in Holland of the spyglass, a device that magnified the image of distant objects. He took this idea and skilfully developed a much more powerful instrument, the telescope, with a much greater magnification. He then used this to study the heavens. He discovered the four moons of Jupiter. He observed the rings of Saturn and the surface of the Moon. He saw that the Milky Way was made up of countless tiny stars. It is claimed that, within two months of using the telescope, he made more discoveries that changed the world than anyone has ever made before or since.

At that time, the common belief was that the Earth was the centre of the universe and that the heavenly bodies revolved around it. Galileo's observations supported the theory of the Polish monk Copernicus, who claimed that Earth and all other planets revolve around the Sun.

After Galileo published a book about his astronomy discoveries and his belief in a Sun-centred Universe, he was called to Rome to answer charges brought against him by the Inquisition. He was cleared of charges of heresy, but made to promise not to promote the heliocentric theory of the solar system. In 1632, he published a book supporting this theory and was condemned by the church. He was exiled to remain in his own house. From there, he continued to publish scientific papers – even after he went blind in 1637. He died in 1642.

In 1992, 350 years after Galileo's death, Pope John Paul II admitted that errors had been made by the Catholic Church in the case of Galileo.

INSIGHTS FOR INNOVATORS

Build on the inventions of others. Galileo took the humble spyglass and turned it into a mighty telescope. He took the ideas of Copernicus and refined them into a more complete understanding of the solar system.

Trust experiments. At a time when people held fixed views rooted in religion and upbringing, Galileo sought to understand the universe by experiment. Furthermore, if the experiment proved his theory wrong, then he was capable of learning and changing his mind. Great innovators prefer experiments to supposition.

Run the numbers. Galileo, unlike many experimenters of the day, believed that Science had to be based on Mathematics. In this regard, he was in the tradition of Archimedes, Pythagoras and (after him) Newton and Einstein. He would validate a hypothesis with mathematical analysis. Innovators relish real-world data and analysis because, from them, they can gain insights and deeper understanding.

GOVINDAPPA VENKATASWAMY

(1918 – 2006)

Indian eye surgeon and founder of the
Aravind Eye Hospitals

How could a crippled doctor improve the lives of thousands of poor people?

Govindappa Venkataswamy was born in 1918 in Vadamalapuram, India. He studied at the American College, Madurai and then at the Government Ophthalmic Hospital, Madras, where he qualified as an ophthalmologist.

In his twenties he served with the Indian Army as a doctor, but had to retire because he suffered from severe rheumatoid arthritis. His fingers were crippled, he had difficulty standing and he suffered great pain. He endured and survived these afflictions. Despite the arthritis in his hands, he became a skilled eye surgeon.

In 1956, he became the Head of the Department of Ophthalmology at the Madurai Medical College. Over the next 20 years, he and his team carried out over 100,000 successful eye surgeries. He started a programme of mobile clinics to take eye treatment and cataract surgery to remote villages. He lobbied the prime minister of India, Mrs Indira Gandhi, to set up a national organisation to treat blindness.

In 1977, at the age of 58, Venkataswamy founded the Aravind Eye Hospital in Madurai, whose mission is to 'to eradicate needless blindness'. He had been fascinated by the automation processes in car assembly plants and fast-food chains, such as McDonald's. He came to believe that he could introduce a similar process for the rapid treatment of cataracts. Using this approach towards surgical processes, he has developed his clinic in Madurai into one of the largest facilities in the world for eye care. His clinic provides free eye care to two-thirds of its patients from the revenue generated from its one-third of paying patients.

He trained paramedics to do 70 per cent of the work required in each surgery, freeing up doctors to perform the more demanding tasks. He brought assembly line thinking to the process and reduced the cost of each cataract operation to around $10 (compared with, say, $1,600 in the USA). Each surgeon carries out some 2,600 operations a year (compared with 250 in most other hospitals and countries).

INSIGHTS FOR INNOVATORS

Copy an idea from elsewhere and bring it into your field. Venkataswamy copied the assembly line idea from car manufacturing and fast food restaurants and applied it to cataract operations. He made the process so fast and cheap that it became available to the many thousands of Indians suffering from cataracts.

You are never too old to start changing the world. Venkataswamy was 58 when he started his innovative eye hospital. At that age, many people would be thinking about retiring from work, especially if they suffered from arthritis. But Venkataswamy chose to launch a major innovation in order to help poor people across India to see better.

DID YOU KNOW?... In Aravind Hospitals, a typical operating room has two tables side by side. A support team prepares one table with a patient, while the surgeon is working on the other. As soon as he or she finishes, the surgeon simply turns around and starts surgery on the other table.

JOSEPH LISTER

(1827 – 1912)

Surgeon who pioneered antiseptic surgery

In 1865, an 11-year-old boy, James Greenlees, was run over by a cart in Glasgow. He was rushed to the Royal Infirmary with a gashed leg, containing a multiple fracture. The normal outcome of this kind of injury at the time was either amputation or death through infection (or sometimes both). Fortunately for Greenlees, the surgeon who treated him was Joseph Lister, who had some radical ideas about infection.

At that time, doctors thought that infection or sepsis, as it was known, was caused by bad air. But Lister had studied the work of French scientist Louis Pasteur, who had found that organisms in the air caused food to rot. Lister thought that similar organisms might cause sepsis in wounds. He had also learnt that Frederick Calvert, a Manchester chemistry professor, had discovered that carbolic acid delayed the decay of corpses. Lister reasoned that the acid might kill the organisms.

Lister dressed the wound of Greenlees with lint dipped in carbolic acid and put splints on the broken leg. Four days later, Lister removed the dressing to examine the wound. Normally, he would encounter the smell of rotting flesh from a four-day-old wound, but this time there was no infection. The wound was clean. After six weeks, the bones knitted back together and Greenlees recovered.

Lister published this finding and several others in the eminent medical journal *The Lancet*. He went on to recommend fundamental changes to the process of surgery through the use of sterilisation. In those days, surgeons saw no need to wash their hands, tools or aprons during surgery. Lister recommended that operating theatres and staff were scrupulously clean. He developed a carbolic acid spray that could be used on patients' wounds.

Although there was initial resistance from doctors, Lister's recommendations were adopted gradually throughout Britain and the world. Sterilisation of surgical instruments became standard practice and this led to a vast reduction in post-operative infections. Countless lives were saved.

Lister became professor of medicine at Edinburgh University and continued to study and write on antiseptic procedures. He retired in 1893. However, on 24 August 1902, the King of England, Edward VII, was struck down with appendicitis just two days before his coronation. The surgeons involved asked for Lister's help and he advised them on the most advanced antiseptic surgical methods. They followed these procedures and the operation was a success. The King later said to Lister, 'I know that if it had not been for you and your work, I wouldn't be sitting here today.'

INSIGHTS FOR
INNOVATORS

Read widely in your subject area. Find out what other leading researchers and thinkers in your field are doing and see if you can build on their ideas to develop your own innovations. Lister's reading of the work of Pasteur and Calvert led to his deduction that carbolic acid could prevent infections.

Try it out. Lister did not just theorise about the use of antiseptic methods. He tried them on James Greenlees and many others. The data from these cases helped prove his argument and convince the medical authorities to take notice.

DID YOU KNOW?... The antiseptic mouthwash Listerine is named in honour of Joseph Lister. It was developed in 1879 by Joseph Lawrence, a chemist in St Louis, Missouri. This long-lived brand is owned by Johnson & Johnson.

MARIE CURIE

(1867 – 1934)

The only double Nobel Prizewinner
in different sciences

Maria Sklodowska was born in Warsaw at a time when Poland was occupied by Russia. Her parents were teachers who were punished for supporting Polish independence. She was a brilliant student and read voraciously, but she was not allowed to go to university in Poland. She took a job as a governess in order to save some money. She became involved in a students' revolutionary organisation and found it necessary to leave the country. In 1891, she moved to Paris to study Science at the Sorbonne. There she met Pierre Curie, a professor of Physics. They were married in 1895 and she adopted the French form of her name – Marie.

The Curies worked together to investigate the recently observed phenomenon of radioactivity. In 1898, they announced the discovery of a new chemical element, Polonium, which Marie named after her home country. Later that year, they discovered another new element, Radium. They were awarded the Nobel Prize for Physics in 1903.

Pierre was killed in a traffic accident in 1906. Marie continued the work they had started. She became the first woman professor to teach at the Sorbonne. She received a second Nobel Prize, this time for Chemistry, in 1911, for her work in researching radioactivity.

Marie Curie was the first woman to win a Nobel Prize, the first person and only woman to win twice and the only person to win twice in different sciences.

Curie developed the theory of radioactivity – a term that she invented. Her research led to techniques for isolating radioactive isotopes and for the use of X-rays in surgery. During the First World War, she helped to equip ambulances with X-ray equipment and, at times, she drove these to the front lines. She trained doctors in the use of X-rays and she became head of the radiological service at the International Red Cross.

Little was known at the time about the dangers of radiation and Curie suffered painful burns from handling radium. She died in

1934 from leukaemia, caused by exposure to high-energy radiation from her research.

INSIGHTS FOR
INNOVATORS

Face down the difficulties. Few scientists can have worked under more difficult circumstances than the Curies. They spent most of their money on apparatus and materials. Often, they did not have enough to eat. Their laboratory was a cold and draughty shed. In addition, Marie continued to face great opposition from male scientists around the world who were sceptical that a woman could do such work.

Have a higher purpose – the innovation is the reward. Although she was poor, Marie Curie disdained financial awards and gave money away to those less fortunate. When the First World War started, she tried to donate her gold Nobel medals to the French war effort, but the offer was refused. She was admired for her honesty and modest lifestyle – even when she became famous. She refused to patent her discoveries with radium, preferring the benefits to go to medical science. In 1929, she was granted $50,000 by US well-wishers and she promptly donated it all to the Warsaw Radium Institute. For Marie Curie, her contribution to the advancement of science was reward enough.

DID YOU KNOW ?... Marie Curie's papers, dating back to the 1890s, and even her cookbook, are considered too dangerous to handle because they are still highly radioactive. Her papers are kept in lead-lined boxes and researchers who want to examine them must wear protective clothing.

PART 8
VISIONARY

ELON MUSK

(BORN 1971)

Serial entrepreneur and founder
of Tesla Motors and SpaceX

Elon Musk was born in South Africa. He got his first computer at the age of eight and started to program. At 17, he went to University in Canada and, subsequently, settled in the USA where he founded a company, Zip2, which provided online travel guides. In the early days of the internet book, Zip2 was a success and, in 1999, he sold it to Compaq Computer Corporation for $330 million. Straight away, Musk started another internet company, X.com, to provide online payments. It became PayPal and he held 11 per cent of the stock when it was sold to eBay in 2002 for $1.5 billion.

In the same year, Musk founded his third company, Space Exploration Technologies Corporation, or SpaceX, to build commercial vehicles for space travel. In 2008, NASA chose SpaceX to transport cargo to the International Space Station (ISS). In 2012, SpaceX made history when it became the first commercial company to send a rocket into space carrying a payload to the ISS.

In 2004, Musk had helped fund the start-up Tesla Motors in order to produce mass-market electric cars. In 2008, he became CEO and product architect. In the same year, the company launched its Roadster, an electric sports car powered by a lithium ion battery. In 2010, Tesla Motors raised $226 million in its initial public offering. Musk has helped shape the company's many innovations. It was he who insisted on a carbon-fibre-reinforced polymer body. He took the unprecedented step of opening all the company's electric car patents to outside use saying, 'We will not initiate patent lawsuits against anyone who, in good faith, wants to use our technology.' Unlike other automobile manufacturers, Tesla Motors sells direct to the public rather than using dealerships.

In 2013, Musk proposed a radical new concept for transportation, the 'Hyperloop', which would transport people at speeds of up to 700 mph through pods in low-pressure tubes. He has funded development of the idea and, in 2015, he announced a competition for designs for a Hyperloop pod prototype.

He has expounded grand ideas on the potential of space exploration for the benefit and survival of the human race. To this end, he created the Musk Foundation, to advance space exploration and the development of clean, renewable sources of energy.

INSIGHTS FOR INNOVATORS

Think big. Elon Musk is not interested in just starting successful companies. He has a vision of space exploration for the benefit of mankind. He wants to find radically new and cleaner ways of transporting people. In his own way, he wants to use science and entrepreneurship to make the world a better place. He has set out to make a big impact. If you have a big vision, then it can inspire people and give you and your team a stronger sense of purpose and value.

Bypass the normal channels. Tesla Motors sells direct to end-users. It has 'galleries' in shopping malls rather than expansive dealer showrooms. It makes all its patent innovation transparent and available to others. It is refreshingly different from conventional car companies and this increases its appeal to people who want an unconventional and cleaner car.

Use one success to build another. Musk did not settle back after selling his first internet start-up. When he made his first millions, he did not retire to a villa on the beach. He used his early successes to fuel his big ambitions. If you have an early victory, then use it as a platform for further bigger and bolder ventures.

JOHN F. KENNEDY

(1917 – 1963)

US President

On 25 May 1961, President John F. Kennedy announced to a joint session of Congress the remarkable and ambitious goal of sending a man to the moon. His famous words were, 'I believe that this nation should commit itself to achieving the goal, before this decade is out, of landing a man on the Moon and returning him safely to the Earth. No single space project in this period will be more impressive to mankind, or more important in the long-range exploration of space; and none will be so difficult or expensive to accomplish.'

When, in 1960, he became the 35th President of the USA, John Fitzgerald Kennedy was, at the age of 43, the youngest man ever elected to the presidency, the first born in the twentieth century and the first Roman Catholic. He came to office with a dynamic plan to end poverty and ignorance at home and to boost the USA's prestige and standing abroad. By 1961, Kennedy felt that the USA had to catch up and overtake the Soviet Union in the space race. It was a matter of national prestige. The Russians had been the first to put a satellite into space and, in April 1961, they were the first to put a man into space, Yuri Gagarin.

Kennedy knew that he was setting an enormous, costly and risky challenge. He stressed the importance and difficulty of the objective. In 1962, he said, 'We choose to go to the moon in this decade and do the other things, not because they are easy, but because they are hard, because that goal will serve to organize and measure the best of our energies and skills, because that challenge is one that we are willing to accept, one we are unwilling to postpone, and one which we intend to win.'

Kennedy's goal was achieved on 20 July 1969, when Apollo 11 commander Neil Armstrong stepped onto the Moon's surface. It was less than six years after Kennedy's tragic assassination.

Throw down an audacious goal. At the time Kennedy gave his speech committing the USA to a moon landing, there had been no spacewalk, no docking in space and no lunar module had been designed. It was a tremendous and uncertain undertaking. He did not underestimate the difficulty of the challenge, but he stressed to the people of the USA that it was a matter of pride, ambition and security. He appealed to the pioneering heritage of the nation.

Assemble a great team and let them get on with it. While Kennedy's speeches galvanised the nation, NASA hired some of the best and brightest engineers and scientists to start the job. They had a clear goal with a pressing deadline and the freedom and resources to solve the problem. They achieved the historic moon landing within the decade.

None of us has the power and authority that Kennedy had. But, no matter how small your team, it is important to give them a clear and worthwhile purpose. Sit down with your team and agree the challenge and then empower them by asking for their ideas on how to achieve it. Often, it is better to let them try their best ideas rather than imposing your own.

MAHATMA GANDHI

(1869 – 1948)

The visionary who led India
to independence

Mohandas Gandhi is revered by Indians as the Mahatma or 'great soul' who led them to independence from British rule. His humility, principles and actions have been admired by peoples all around the world.

Gandhi was born in Porbandar, India in 1869. He was brought up as a strict Hindu and, as a boy, he promised his mother that he would never eat meat, smoke tobacco or drink alcohol. He kept this promise throughout his life and eschewed all other luxuries, too. At the age of 19, he was sent to London to study law and, subsequently, he worked as a lawyer in India.

Following his training, he went to South Africa in 1893 to help an Indian company. He was appalled at the way in which Indians in South Africa were treated by white people. He stayed there for 21 years, fighting for the rights of oppressed people. In 1913, he led 2,000 Indians on a protest from Transvaal to Natal in defiance of a South African law forbidding Indians from moving across provinces. He was imprisoned for his troubles.

He returned to India where he campaigned for the rights of the downtrodden: the poor, women and people of lower castes. In 1918, he became leader of the National Congress, an independence party. At a time when many believed that a violent revolution was needed, Gandhi advocated passive resistance, opposing government policies without using force. To protest the government monopoly on salt production, he led his followers on a long march to the coast to take salt from the sea.

Another tactic he used was to fast. He would go without food for long periods to protest injustices in British or Indian society. These fasts were dangerous and left him in a weakened state, but he persevered and never lost his sense of humour.

In 1942, he started the 'Quit India' movement at a time when Britain was locked in war with Germany and Japan. He was imprisoned and not released until 1944.

Eventually, his efforts helped lead to the British withdrawal from India in 1947. Much to his distress, this action led to great violence between Hindus and Muslims during the partition of the new states of India and Pakistan.

At an open air prayer meeting for peace, in January 1948, he was shot dead by a Hindu fanatic. His death shocked the world and helped lessen the violence.

He said, 'I shall not fear anyone on earth. I shall not bear ill-will towards anyone. I shall not submit to injustice from anyone. In resisting untruth I shall put up with all suffering.'

INSIGHTS FOR INNOVATORS

You can achieve change through others by becoming a servant leader. Many leaders are flamboyant characters with big egos and a penchant for aggressive action. But that is not necessary. Gandhi showed that he could be a great leader and transform society with humility and passive resistance to injustice.

'Be the change you want to see in the world,' said Gandhi. Many people thought that the only way to remove a colonial power was with violent revolution. Gandhi disagreed with the use of force and believed in non-violent action. He led by example and proved the power of measured and contained rebellion. He inspired people to follow his example and eschew violence. For example, in 2009, President Barack Obama said that his biggest inspiration came from Mahatma Gandhi.

OPRAH WINFREY

(BORN 1954)

The Queen of all media

Oprah Gail Winfrey is a US media mogul, talk show host, actress, producer, philanthropist and spiritual leader. Her TV talk show, *The Oprah Winfrey Show*, was the highest-rated programme ever of its type. She is the first black US billionaire and is seen as the greatest black philanthropist. Many considered her to be the most influential woman in the world. In 2013, she was awarded the Presidential Medal of Freedom by President Barack Obama.

Winfrey was born in 1954 in rural Mississippi to a poor teenage single mother. She had a hard and troubled upbringing. She was sexually abused as a child by a number of male relatives and friends of her mother. At the age of 14, she bore a son who died in infancy.

While still in high school, Oprah took a job at the local radio station and, by the age of 19, she was co-anchoring the local evening news. In 1976, Winfrey moved to Baltimore, where she hosted a hit television chat show, *People Are Talking*. Her fresh, emotional and open-hearted style of hosting became increasingly popular. A Chicago TV station offered her the chance to host her own morning show. *The Oprah Winfrey Show* became a massive hit that ran for 25 seasons, from 1986 to 2011. It was syndicated to over 200 TV stations and more than 100 countries across the world. At the same time, she developed her acting career. She was nominated for an Academy Award for Best Supporting Actress for her role in Steven Spielberg's 1985 film *The Color Purple*. Winfrey launched her own TV network, the Oprah Winfrey Network, in 2011.

She revolutionised the daytime TV talk show with a confessional style of interview that broke taboos. Openly, she discussed issues such as her own sexual abuse and weight loss problems. She espoused gay and lesbian rights. In the 1990s, she reinvented her show with a focus on self-help, literature and spirituality. She launched her book club, which encouraged people to read and boosted the careers of hitherto unknown authors. She supported Barack Obama in his bid for the White House and is credited with adding millions of votes to his campaign. *Life* magazine hailed her the most influential woman of her generation.

She is renowned for her good works and philanthropy. Winfrey's Angel Network has raised more than $50 million for causes ranging from girls' education in South Africa to relief for the victims of Hurricane Katrina. She is an activist for children's rights and proposed a bill to Congress for the naming of child abusers. It became law in 1994.

INSIGHTS FOR INNOVATORS

Try a different and more personal style. Whilst other TV hosts were seen as ingratiating, polished, aggressive or patronising, Winfrey developed her own style, which was warm and open. Because she was candid about her own background and issues, she encouraged people to be truthful and open about theirs.

Embody the change you want to see. Like Gandhi, Winfrey's life exemplifies the values she espouses – particularly openness and empowerment for women and children. You can lead by example to inspire others to change.

Help and become a role model for others. As a woman from a poor background who has overcome disadvantage and abuse, Winfrey has become a role model across the world. Her programme is particularly popular in the Arab world and in Saudi Arabia. Many women there admire her for her modest, yet confident, triumph over adversity.

WALT DISNEY

(1901 – 1966)

Giant of the entertainment industry

As a young man, Walt Disney was fired by a newspaper editor because 'he lacked imagination and had no good ideas'. It was an inauspicious start for a man who went on to be one of the USA's most innovative leaders.

In 1921, he founded his first animation company in Kansas City. It failed. He had to dissolve his company. He could not pay the rent and it is said that he was in such desperate straits he had to eat dog food.

In 1923, Walt and his brother Roy moved to Hollywood to set up a cartoon studio. They had a small success with a cartoon featuring Oswald, the Lucky Rabbit. They followed this up with Mickey Mouse for which Walt himself provided the voice and personality. When Disney offered MGM studios the opportunity to distribute Mickey Mouse films in 1927, he was told that the idea would not work because a giant mouse on the screen would terrify women and children! Mickey Mouse went on to be a huge success.

In 1933, Disney created the most successful cartoon short of all time, *The Three Little Pigs*. It ran continuously in many theatres across the USA. He asked his team what they should do next. The response was more short cartoons featuring pigs – it was a formula that worked. But Disney was more ambitious. He planned something that had never been attempted before – a full length cartoon film. When the film industry learned of Disney's plans to produce an animated feature-length version of *Snow White* in technicolour, they scoffed. People were sure that the project would destroy the Disney Studio and called it 'Disney's Folly'. Both Disney's wife and brother tried to talk him out of the project, but he persisted. Because of Disney's demands for high quality, the film took four years to make and his company nearly ran out of money. The film became the most successful motion picture of 1938 and earned over $8 million on its initial release, a huge amount in those times. Disney won eight Oscars for the film.

Disney continued to innovate and take risks throughout his business career. His film business was remarkably successful, but that was not enough. He wanted to found a theme park in Los Angeles: Disneyland. He told one of his aides, 'I want it to look like nothing else in the world.' It is reported that his project was rejected by 300 bankers before he raised the finance he needed. Why would a banker believe that a film maker could make a success of such a huge, untried and entirely different venture? Disneyland opened in 1955 and was a great success. It was followed by Disney World in Florida, which was designed by Walt Disney and opened in 1971, some five years after Disney's death. It is now the number one holiday resort in the world, with over 50 million visitors every year.

INSIGHTS FOR INNOVATORS

Do not settle for repeating what worked before. Disney was never satisfied with previous success. He wanted to try new, different and bigger ideas.

Ignore the doubters. Believe in yourself. Listen to what the critics say but, often, it is best to go ahead anyway. Disney ignored the doubters and made huge innovations happen.

Have a big vision. A visitor to Disney World some years after Disney's death, said to his son, Roy Disney, 'What a pity your father never lived to see this.' Roy reputedly replied, 'It is here because he saw it.' His ambitious plans inspired his team. Do not settle for small goals – aim for something magnificent.

ZHAO KUANGYIN

(927 – 976)

Emperor of China and founder
of the Song Dynasty

Zhao Kuangyin became the Emperor Taizu and ruled China from 960 until his death in 976. He was the founder of the Song Dynasty and laid the foundations for its longevity and success. It lasted until 1279. He was a triumphant warrior, but also a shrewd ruler and an efficient administrator. China had been weak and fragmented, with power lying between squabbling warlords. He united it into a powerful empire. This realm needed a strong and trustworthy administration and Zhao constructed it by reforming the Chinese civil service.

Appointment to the civil service was highly valued and it had been subject to nepotism, manipulation and corruption. Zhao implemented reforms that eradicated favouritism and bias in the selection process. All candidates had to face two or more written tests and their papers (with the names removed) were marked by three separate examiners. Students would spend years preparing for the exams. Many thousands applied each year, but only a handful of the very best candidates were selected. The Chinese civil service was admired and copied by other nations, most notably by the British, who used a similar system to administer a large empire in the nineteenth century.

Zhao also reformed Chinese political institutions, so as to encourage debate and freedom of thought. He fostered innovation, the advance of science, arts, literature and economic theory. Although he had started his career as a soldier and rose to power in a military coup, he went on to weaken the power of the army and of the warlords. He valued peace rather than war. He ushered in the Song Dynasty during which time China enjoyed economic growth, scientific advance and artistic achievement. This period is considered comparable to the later Renaissance in Europe.

Zhao was born the son of a military commander. As a boy, he was a highly skilled archer and horseman. He had a reputation as a daredevil. In the army, he rose to become a distinguished general. As Emperor, he was a benevolent ruler by the standards of the day. He showed clemency to the enemies he defeated. He would sometimes wander incognito amongst the common people to understand their conditions and issues. He bequeathed a stable and effective government to his heirs, thus laying the foundation for the glories of the Song Dynasty.

INSIGHTS FOR INNOVATORS

Surround yourself with talent. Zhao Kuangyin reformed the examination system by selecting his support staff on academic ability rather than family connections. This enabled him to develop a highly effective bureaucracy that could administer a large empire efficiently and fairly.

Encourage ideas and open debate. Zhao replaced a closed and authoritarian regime with one in which ideas and debate were allowed and facilitated. Every leader needs to hear feedback, criticism and fresh ideas. Few have the courage to do so.

Know the perils that face you and move early to counteract them. The Emperor knew that the most likely threat to his power would come from his own military or from belligerent warlords. He took action to appease them while, at the same time, reducing their powers.

INDEX

actors
  Allen, Woody 35–7
  David Bowie 4–5
  Madonna 20–1
adaption 64
adversity, overcoming 172
age 244
Allen, Woody 35–7
Amazon.com 58–61, 169
Andersen, Hans Christian 10–12
antiseptic surgery 245, 246–7
Apple 48, 180, 181, 182, 183
Aravind Eye Hospitals 242, 243–4
Archimedes 222–4
Archimedes principle 223
architecture, Michelangelo 95
artists
  Dali, Salvador 32–4
  Lichtenstein, Roy 29–31
  Michelangelo 93–6
  Picasso, Pablo 26–8
assembly line thinking, in medicine 244
assumptions, challenging by asking
     questions 237
astronomers, Galileo 209–40
athletes, Fosbury, Dick 188–90
authors
  Allen, Woody 36
  Andersen, Hans Christian 10–12
  Rowling, J.K. 13–15
  Swift, Jonathan 173–6

backwards step to find simpler way 154
Barbier, Charles 133

Baylis, Trevor 152–5
Beethoven, Ludwig van 89–92
Bell, Sir Alexander Graham 114, 218–21
Bell Telephone Company 219, 220
Bernstein, Sidney 75–7
Bezos, Jeff 58–61
Birdseye 50–1
Birdseye, Clarence 49–51
bisexuality, attitudes towards 4
Blue Origin 60
Body Shop, The 159–62
Bohemian Rhapsody 7–8
books
  second-hand book sale – online 59
  virtual bookstores 59
Bowie, David 3–5, 77
Braille, Louis 132–5
braille system 133–5
brand promotion 22
branding 85
Buonarroti, Michelangelo *see* Michelangelo
bureaucracy 71, 209
Busicom 147
business leaders
  Bernstein, Sidney 75–7
  Bezos, Jeff 58–61
  Birdseye, Clarence 49–51
  Dunstone, Sir Charles 78–80
  Honda, Soichiro 81–3
  Kamprad, Ingvar 55–8
  Kroc, Ray 65–7
  McEwen, Rob 72–4
  Morita, Akio 41–4
  Mulcahy, Anne 45–8

business leaders (*continued*)
  Peter, Daniel 52–4
  Ruimin, Zhang 84–6
  Semler, Ricardo 68–71
  Strauss, Levi 62–4
business to business web services 60, 61

Calvert, Frederick 246
cameras, Polaroid 235, 236–7
Cannae, Battle of 168
capacity, unused 61
Captive Flying Machine 116, 117
Carphone Warehouse 79–80
cartoons, Disney, Walt 265–7
cataract operations 231, 243–4
CD players, portable 43
Chain, Ernst 216, 217
change, imposing on yourself 5
childbirth, Odon device 130–1
children, inspiration from 31
China 268–70
chocolate, milk 52–4
Ciccone, Madonna Louise *see* Madonna
cinema industry 76
Clerk, John 172
clocks 121–5
  grasshopper escapement 122
  gridiron pendulum 122
  marine chronometer 123–5
clockwork radio 152–5
clothing industry, jeans 62–4
Cloud infrastructure services 60
collaboration 3–5, 54, 64, 111, 125, 217
comedians, Allen, Woody 35–7
comfort zone, mixing with people
      outside 12
commercial television 76–7
communication, vision 46–7
composers *see* music/musicians
compound pulley 223
computers
  home 139
  IBM PC 163–6
  open architecture – advantages of
      164, 165, 166

computing technologies 48
connection, spotting 131
constraints, as aid to creativity 96
contacts, using 194
controversy 22, 31, 160–1, 162
Cooper, Martin 136–9
cooperation 54
Copernicus 240
creativity 91, 96, 201
Crimean War 192–3
crowdfunding 110, 111
crowdsourcing 73, 74, 122
Cubism 27
culture 57
Curie, Marie 248–50
curiosity 51, 114, 217
customers
  alternative way to reach 169
  learning from 85, 86
  listening to 12
customers' needs 44, 61, 134

Dali, Salvador 32–4
D'Aloisio, Nick 140–2
Darwin, Charles 225–8
  The Origin of Species 226
Davis, Jacob 63
Davis, Miles 23–5
deaf, communication 219
digital natives 142
Disney, Walt 265–7
domestic appliances 85
Dunstone, Sir Charles 78–80

Edison, Thomas 116, 149–51
ego 67
Eiffel, Gustave 198–201
Eiffel Tower 198–201
electric cars 254
electronic books reader 60, 61
electronic goods 42–4
elimination 44
employees
  democracy 69–70
  feedback 71

give freedom and space 148
    management 69
    recruitment 37
    sharing company information
        with 70
    trusting 70
energy, renewable 255
engineers, Eiffel, Gustave 198–201
entertainment industry, Disney,
    Walt 265–7
environmentally friendly approaches
    160–2
equity, retain some 155
Escoffier, Auguste 185–7
Estridge, Don 163–6
ethics 206–9
Eureka moment 224
everyday life, spotting problem in 111
evolution, theory of 225, 226–8
exclusivity 64
experimentation 17, 151, 234, 239
    trusting 197, 240–1
eye surgeon 231, 242–4

failure
    handling 212
    as part of process 164, 166
fast food chain 65–7
film directors, Allen, Woody
    35–7
finance, raising 110, 111, 178
financial management 99
fire sprinkler, automatic 116
Fleming, Alexander 215–17
Florey, Howard 216, 217
focus groups 44, 182
focus on process 67
form and function 180, 181
Fosbury, Dick 188–90
Fosbury Flop 188–90
franchising innovation 15
Freeplay Energy 153–4
frozen food industry 49–51
furniture, IKEA 55–8
fusion 25

Galapagos Islands 226
Galileo 238–41
Gandhi, Mohandas 259–61
gap in market, spotting 79, 80
geometrical theorems 224
'gig economy' 211, 212
Globe Theatre 104, 105
goals, audacious 257–8
gold mining 72–4
Grameen Bank 206, 207–8
gramophone 150
Granada Television 76, 77
Grant, R. *Contemporary Strategy
    Analysis* 21
graphical form, using 231
gun, machine 115–17

Haier 85
Hannibal 167–9
'harmony of the spheres' 101
Harry Potter see Rowling, J.K.
Haydn, Joseph, on Mozart 99
health management 99
helping others by innovation 179
high jump, Fosbury Flop 188–90
hire and ride-sharing services, Uber 210,
    211–12
HMS *Beagle* 226
Hoff, Marcian Edward (Ted) 146–8
Honda Motor Corporation 81–3
Honda, Soichiro 81–3
hospitals, nursing – Florence Nightingale
    191–4
hydraulic screw 223
Hyperloop 254
hypothesis, validation by mathematical
    analysis 241

IBM PC 163–6
Ibuka, Masru 42
ideas 227–8
    adaption of concept that works
        elsewhere 51, 244
    building on ideas of others 240, 247
    copying from nature 114, 220

ideas (*continued*)
  make existing idea better 134
  radical 131
  recombinations of existing 120
  testing 15, 17, 197, 231, 240–1
IKEA 55–8
improvisation 17
inconvenience, as opportunity
    for innovation 237
incubators 110
India, Gandhi's influence 260–1
industrial research laboratory 150
Innocentive.com xi
Intel 147
intellectual property, protection 51, 155,
  221
internet commerce, Amazon 58–61
internet entrepreneurs 140–2
intuition 80
inventors
  Baylis, Trevor 152–5
  Braille, Louis 132–5
  Cooper, Martin 136–9
  D'Aloisio, Nick 140–2
  Edison, Thomas 149–51
  Gutenberg, Johannes 118–20
  Harrison, John 121–5
  Hoff, Ted 146–8
  Maxim, Sir Hiram 115–17
  Mestral, George de 112–14
  Migicovsky, Eric 109–11
  Odón, Jorge 129–31
  Sipe, John 126–8
  Spencer, Percy 143–5
Ive, Jonathan 181

jazz, Davis, Miles 23–5
jeans 62–4
Jenner, Edward 232–4
Jobs, Steve 48, 180–2
Judkins, Rod, *The Art of Creative
  Thinking* 175

Kalanick, Travis 210–12
Kamprad, Ingvar 55–8

Kennedy, John F. 256–8
Kickstarter 110
Kindle 60, 61
Kroc, Ray 65–7
Kuangyin, Zhao 268–70

Lamarr, Hedy 202–5
Land, Edwin 235–7
launch of idea, use of brazen stunt 138
leading by example 264
learning from customers 85, 86
Lennon, John 16–18
levers 223
Lichtenstein, Roy 29–31, 176
lightbulb 116
lights, electric 116
listening skills 47
Lister, Joseph 245–7
Listerine 247
longitude, marine chronometer 123–5
Longitude Act 122
Longitude Prize 122, 124
longitude problem 122–5

McCartney, Paul 16–18
McDonald's 65–7
McEwen, Rob 72–4
machine gun 115–17
Madonna 19–22
managers
  evaluation by subordinates 71
  recruitment 71
Marconi, Guglielmo 195–7
marine chronometer 123–5
mass media, using to gain exposure
  155
mass production 150
mathematicans
  Archimedes 222–4
  Galileo 209–40
  Pythagoras 100–2
  Maxim, Sir Hiram 115–17
media industry 75–7
  using 194
  Winfrey, Oprah 262–4

Mendeleev, Dmitri 229–31
Mercury, Freddie 6–9
Mestral, George de 112–14
Michelangelo 93–6
microcredit/microloans 206, 207–9
microprocessor 146–8
microwave oven 143–5
Migicovsky, Eric 109–11
military strategists, Hannibal 167–9
mining industry, gold 72–4
mobile phone 136–9
mobile phone app, Summly 141
mobile phone retailer 78–80
moon landing 257, 258
moral purpose 206–9
Morita, Akio 41–4
motor car industry 81–3
motorbikes 82, 83
Motorola 137, 138
move to where action is in your
        speciality 197
Mozart, Wolfgang Amadeus 97–9
Mulcahy, Anne 45–8
music/musicians
    Allen, Woody 36
    Beethoven, Ludwig van 89–92
    Bowie, David 3–5
    Davis, Miles 23–5
    Lennon, John 16–18
    McCartney, Paul 16–18
    Madonna 19–22
    Mercury, Freddie 6–9
    Mozart, Wolfgang Amadeus 97–9
Musk, Elon 253–5

nature, copying idea from 114, 220
Nelson, Viscount Horatio 170–2
Nestlé Company 53, 54
Nestlé, Henri 53
networks 125
NeXT 181
Nightingale, Florence 191–4
Nobel Prize winners
    Chain, Ernst 216, 217
    Curie, Marie 248–50
    Fleming, Alexander 215–17
    Florey, Howard 216, 217
    Yunus, Muhammad 206–9
notoriety 175, 176
Noyce, Robert 147, 148
nursing, Nightingale, Florence 191–4

Odon device 129, 130–1
Odón, Jorge 129–31
open architecture 164, 165, 166
open debate 270
open source software 73, 74
opinion leaders, lobbying 226–7
opposite, do the 161
Oprah Winfey Show, The 263–4
Orange Aids 153
outsider
    benefits of being 83, 131
    thinking like 74

partnerships, benefits of 18
passion, demonstrating with action 86
Pasteur, Louis 246
patents 51, 155, 221
patience 135, 145
patterns, using to predict results 231
PayPal 254
Pebble Technology 109–11
peer-to-peer file-sharing 211
pendulum, use to measure time 239
penicillin 215, 216–17
people management 69
periodic table 229, 230–1
persistance 125
personal intervention 194
Peter, Daniel 52–4
philosophers, Pythagoras 100–2
physicists, Galileo 209–40
Picasso, Pablo 26–8
pie charts 194
Pixar 181
playwrights, Shakespeare, William 103–5
point of attack, changing 171, 172
Polaroid camera 235, 236–7
Polaroid technology, applications 236

Polonium 249
Pop Art Movement 29–31
poverty, alleviation 207, 209
practice, need for 18
precision 201
printing press 118
problem
    approaching from different direction
        190
    looking for better way to solve 148
    looking for solution within 117
    as opportunity for innovation 142
process, rearranging sequence 187
product innovation, Sony Corporation
        42–4
protection of invention 155, 221
public relations, powers of 137
publicity, generating through activism
        and controversy 160–1, 162
Pythagoras 100–2

quality 85
Queen 7–8

radio
    clockwork 152–5
    pioneer – Marconi 195–7
    signals – use of spread spectrum 203–4
    transistor 42
radioactivity, theory of 249
Radium 249
Raytheon 144
reaction, prepare for 226
rearrange existing order 231
Red Swoosh 211
redesign 125
reinvention 21, 28
rejection, handling 14, 15
reskilling 145
resources, innovate with other people's
        212
restauranteurs
    Escoffier, Auguste 185–7
    Romano, Phil 177–9
restaurants

fast food 65–7
    McDonald's 65–7
rights of oppressed people 260
risk 51
    estimation of downside 80
Roberts, Ed 139
Roddick, Anita 159–62
role model 264
Romano, Phil 177–9
Rowling, J.K. 13–15
    Harry Potter 13–15
Ruimin, Zhang 84–6
rules, breaking 165

satire 173–6
Savoy Hotel 186–7
scientific trials 151
scientists
    Archimedes 222–4
    Bell, Alexander Graham 114, 218–21
    Curie, Marie 248–50
    Darwin, Charles 225–8
    Fleming, Alexander 215–17
    Galileo 238–41
    Jenner, Edward 232–4
    Land, Edwin 235–7
    Lister, Joseph 245–7
    Mendeleev, Dmitri 229–31
    Venkataswamy, Govindappa 242–4
Scour Inc 211
sculpture, Michelangelo 94
self-belief 33, 67, 92, 267
self-organising teams 86
Semler, Ricardo 68–71
serendipity 145
serial entrepreneurs
    Musk, Elon 253–5
    Romano, Phil 177–9
Shakespeare, William 103–5
shoe soles, siping 127
shoes, 'electric' 154
showman 197
singers
    David Bowie 3–5
    Lennon, John 16–18

McCartney, Paul 16–18
Madonna 19–22
Mercury, Freddie 6–9
siping process 126–8
Sistine Chapel, Vatican 94–5, 96
smallpox vaccine 232, 233–4
social activism 160–1
Sony Corporation 41, 42–4
Sony Walkman 43, 44
South Africa 260
space exploration 60, 254, 255, 257–8
SpaceX 253, 254
Spencer, Percy 143–5
standards, setting high 182, 187
Star Trek 137, 138, 139
Statue of Liberty 200
sterilisation, surgical instruments 246–7
stock ticker 150
storylines, borrowing and developing
     104, 105
Strauss, Levi 62–4
streamline processes 67
style icons, David Bowie 3–5
styles, experimenting with new 20
Surrealism 27
Swift, Jonathan 173–6

tape players, Sony Walkman 43, 44
teams
   assembling 258
   empowering 258
   inspiring 172
   mixed skills 151
teamwork, large-scale 150
telephone 218, 219–21
telescope 239–40
television broadcasting 76–7
televisions 43
tenacity 125
Tesla Motors 253, 254
testing idea 231
   by experiment 15, 17, 197, 234, 239,
     240–1
theme parks, Disneyland 267

threats to your business 54
time, measurement by pendulum 239
Tokyo Telecommunications Engineering
     Company 42
Tomorrow's World 153
touch screen 182
Trafalgar, Battle of 171, 172
Trasimeno, Battle of 168
travel 101, 102
Trebia, Battle of 168
Trevor Bayliss Brands 154
tyres, siping 127

Uber 210, 211–12
unpredictability 179
US President, Kennedy, John F. 256–8

vaccines, smallpox 232, 233–4
vehicles, Uber 210, 211–12
Velcro 112–14
Venkataswamy, Govindappa 231, 242–4
Vickers Ltd 116
video recorders 43
view, taking different 131
vision 267
   communicating 46–7

Wallace, Alfred 226
watches, 'smart', Pebble Techology 110
Western Union 220
Winfrey, Oprah 262–4
words, invention of new 104, 105
Wozniak, Steve 181
writers see authors; playwrights

x-rays 249
X.com 254
Xerox Corporation 45–8
Xerox Palo Alto Research Centre 48

Y Combinator 110

Ziggy Stardust see Bowie, David
Zip2 254